Society as a
Department Store

RELIGION, POLITICS, AND SOCIETY IN THE NEW MILLENNIUM

Series Editors: Michael Novak, American Enterprise Institute, and Brian C. Anderson, Manhattan Institute

For nearly five centuries, it was widely believed that moral questions could be resolved through reason. The Enlightenment once gave us answers to these perennial questions, but the answers no longer seem adequate. It has become apparent that reason alone is not enough to answer the questions that define and shape our existence. Many now believe that we have come to the edge of the Enlightenment and are stepping forth into a new era, one that may be the most religious we have experienced in five hundred years. This series of books explores this new historical condition, publishing important works of scholarship in various disciplines that help us to understand the trends in thought and belief we have come from and to define the ones toward which we are heading.

Political Memoirs, by Aurel Kolnai, edited by Francesca Murphy

Challenging the Modern World: Karol Wojtyla/John Paul II and the Development of Catholic Social Teaching, by Samuel Gregg

The Scepter Shall Not Depart from Judah: Perspectives on the Persistence of the Political in Judaism, by Alan L. Mittleman

In the World, But Not of the World: Christian Social Teaching at the End of the Twentieth Century, by Andrew L. Fitz-Gibbon

The Surprising Pope: Understanding the Thought of John Paul II, by Maciej Zieba, O.P.

A Free Society Reader: Principles for the New Millennium, edited by Michael Novak, William Brailsford, and Cornelis Heesters

Beyond Self Interest: A Personalist Approach to Human Action, Gregory R. Beabout, et al.

Human Nature and the Discipline of Economics: Personalist Anthropology and Economic Methodology, Patricia Donohue-White, et al.

The Free Person and the Free Economy: A Personalist View of Market Economics, Anthony J. Santelli Jr., et al.

Meaninglessness: The Solutions of Nietzsche, Freud, and Rorty, by M. A. Casey

Boston's Cardinal: Bernard Law, the Man and His Witness, edited by Romanus Cessario, O.P.

Don't Play Away Your Cards, Uncle Sam: The American Difference, by Olof Murelius, edited by Jana Novak

Society as a Department Store: Critical Reflections on the Liberal State, by Ryszard Legutko

Society as a Department Store

Critical Reflections on the Liberal State

Ryszard Legutko

LEXINGTON BOOKS
Lanham • Boulder • New York • Oxford

LEXINGTON BOOKS

Published in the United States of America
by Lexington Books
A Member of the Rowman & Littlefield Publishing Group
4720 Boston Way, Lanham, Maryland 20706
www.rowmanlittlefield.com

PO Box 317
Oxford
OX2 9RU, UK

British Library Cataloguing in Publication Information Available

Library of Congress Cataloging-in-Publication Data

Legutko, Ryszard, 1949–
  Society as a department store : critical reflections on the liberal state / Ryszard Legutko.
    p. cm.—(Religion, politics, and society in the new millennium)
  Includes bibliographical references and index.
  ISBN 0-7391-0371-7 (cloth : alk. paper)
  1. Liberalism. I. Title. II. Series.

JC574.L44 2002
320.51—dc21

2002004444

Printed in the United States of America

♾™ The paper used in this publication meets the minimum requirements of
American National Standard for Information Sciences—Permanence of Paper
for Printed Library Materials, ANSI/NISO Z39.48–1992.

Contents

Introduction

The essays that constitute this book were written on various occasions, but they were motivated, in the arguments they refute as well as in those they put forward, by the same experience—the experience of living in a society that suffered several decades of totalitarianism and then, finally liberated, became a part of the free world of nations. But that is not all. These essays also arise from the experience of someone who has enjoyed the blessings of a free society—who sees the abolition of communism as one of mankind's most beneficial events—yet who cannot help feeling a certain disillusionment at what the newly regained freedom has brought.

And not one disillusionment, but two. The first came from the conviction I formed in Poland in the decade before the fall of communism that the intellectual class would long avoid any inclination to progressive ideologies. I even thought, somewhat hubristically, that if any message might be exported from this part of Europe and be of value to the outside world, it would be a deeper understanding of communism and communist temptations, and of any ideology that might find inspiration from similar tendencies of human nature. Unfortunately, this was not to be the case. Not only do many Poles tend to forget about communism, but even worse, we have witnessed in Central Europe in general, and in Poland in particular, a remarkable presence of anti-anticommunist attitudes. To my surprise, communism is no longer an object of interest; the only reaction it receives is indifference or mild reproach, perhaps from the assumption that as an ideological and political system it has been irrevocably overcome. On the other hand, anticommunism has begun to be treated in a much harsher way, presumably because it is viewed as an unnecessarily

1

rigorous posture that stands in the way of progressive ideas and new ideologies that are filling in the social and political space emptied by Marxism and its ideological allies. As a result, Poland has long ceased to be the
place where the lessons of history are interpreted; it more and more resembles Western societies where people turn away from history and
where anticommunists rather than communists are feared by large segments of society, precisely because the former are believed to be too much
preoccupied with the past, while the latter, having turned overnight into
social democrats or egalitarian liberals, claim as always to be working for
progress and the welfare of all.

My second disillusionment concerns the reception of liberalism (understood as a system of general ideas, not as a specific project of economic reform). I expected, perhaps naïvely, that in the new era liberalism would
be an instrument through which it would be easier to understand our experience, both collective and individual, and to deliberate with one another about the ends we pursue and the best means to them. It turned out
that liberalism was perceived not merely as a system of procedures but
rather as the ultimate goal of political and social action. Hence the imme-
diate effect of liberalism was not the beginning of a new and lively discussion about the most significant issues, but a rapid growth of intellectual clichés, often accompanied by moralistic rhetoric. The paradox is that
liberalism has led to the weakening of critical thinking and brought about
the degradation of public discourse. To my surprise I have noted that the
categories that determine today's discourse—such as "pluralism," "toleration," "human rights," "freedom of expression," "dialogue," and other
general concepts—do not raise the debate to a new and more interesting
level, but serve as convenient tools to silence opponents. Liberal demonology—the belief that all metaphysically and epistemologically
weighty concepts are politically dangerous and contain seeds of discrimination and repression—has paralyzed people's minds. Instead of making
up intellectually for what we missed while living in the shadow of censorship and Marxist ideology for forty-five years, we have become intimidated, this time without political coercion, and have all too readily
agreed to what we have been hearing with monotonous regularity,
namely, that certain categories are dangerous, that some philosophical
theories have become anachronistic, and that others have to be sacrificed
as we march to join the ranks of the modern or postmodern world. Paradoxically, liberalism has spread the feeling of intellectual impotence and
helplessness, not courage and self-confidence, and made acquiescence to
the ruling clichés a higher form of wisdom.

All the essays here except one do not refer to the Central European situation directly; they do so rather indirectly. I have tried to trace the ideas
that dominate Central European societies to the drama that has been play-

ing out in modern culture. If my reading of the Polish situation is correct, the real actors are elsewhere. To a large degree we depend—"we" being the Polish, Czech, Hungarian, Slovak societies in general, not individuals who have the freedom to use their minds—on what emanates from present-day Western culture. It is essential to understand this drama and to see where the ideas that determine today's thinking came from and what they really mean. It is also essential to keep close contact with the great tradition of Western culture that so many modern and postmodern ideologies declare finished, exhausted, or repressive. As I argue in a piece on Plato published in this volume, the situation of people in modern societies resembles that of ancient Athenians during a conflict between sophists and philosophers, but in a different sense from the one invoked by those who frequently make use of this analogy today: The people of the modern world, like citizens of the democratic *polis*, have the tendency to appeal more and more to general concepts, and less and less to inherited practices, while having little understanding of those concepts. Poles, Czechs, Slovaks, and Hungarians are especially tempted to indulge this tendency, because the majority of them believe they must quickly import modern ideas that they then treat as finished products of the mental work done by others—as, so to speak, commodities that can be purchased and shipped, not as the sorts of things that must be laboriously reconstructed and rethought through their own intellectual effort.

Despite this thoughtlessness with which Western culture is received in Central Europe, I believe the Poles, Czechs, Hungarians, Slovaks, and Bulgarians—at least some of them—have something to contribute to the debate. As a result of living under a system that came into being through a totalitarian revolution, a lot of us have become suspicious of the ideological, political, philosophical, and cultural revolutions that have shaken our societies and our minds during the last two centuries, and which have been particularly destructive during the post-war period. The Central European paradox is that after liberating ourselves from the revolutionary system we have been thrown into a modern Western culture in which revolutionary thinking and revolutionary chic are very much present. After liberating ourselves from the ideology whose functionaries put a large part of the cultural heritage of the Western world into the dustbin of history, we have found ourselves in a culture in which the dustbin of history seems to be very much in use. After liberating ourselves from the system that used all its ideological and political apparatus to destroy classical metaphysics and epistemology, we have now entered a culture in which the struggle against this metaphysics and epistemology is the task of the day.

It should not, then, be surprising that a lot of us Central Europeans are skeptical of, at times even hostile to, the emancipatory rhetoric that flows abundantly from modern culture and modern political theory—rhetoric that we think expresses intellectual hubris rather than genuine humane concerns. We find little appeal both in the postmodern claim that all metaphysics and epistemology are political, and in the liberal claim that one can construct a metaphysically transparent and infinitely spacious political order. If I am not mistaken, many Central Europeans still have faith in the wisdom of classical Western culture, a faith that modern Western culture appears not only to be losing but to be proudly making this loss a central point of its identity.

Let me conclude these introductory remarks by expressing my gratitude to all those who made the publication of this collection of essays possible. I particularly thank Professor Michael Novak and Dr. Brian Anderson for their interest in my work and for encouragement and assistance in the preparation of this volume and Scott Walter for his line editing of the manuscript.

1

+

Society as a
Department Store

To choose is usually painful, but to live without choosing is impossible. This unpardonably banal insight lay at the root of Western political theory; the basic question this theory addressed—how people should organize the life of a community—was closely related to the question of how and what people should choose and, consequently, why some choices are preferable to others. We know that only in a utopia can people be exempted from the unpleasantness of selecting some goals at the expense of others and from the risk of error, whereas in all actually existing political systems we are compelled by nature and by the logic of human affairs to sacrifice some goods in order to achieve others. The obvious means to facilitate the political and social processes of selection was to find a generally valid criterion; it was hoped that, having understood the principle of choice, we would do the right thing and would not feel frustrated by the consequences. Such a criterion should serve as a guideline for all political agents, individual and collective, as well as for the present and future organizers of political orders.

The ancient thinkers had a clear solution to this problem. They argued—and by "they" I mean Plato and Aristotle—that there is an objective hierarchy of goods, and that the polity should strive for the highest good, that is, the highest ethical purpose. Politics, as Aristotle put in the *Nicomachean Ethics,* was "the master science," the science that "uses the rest of the sciences and . . . legislates as to what we are to do and what we are to abstain from; the end of this science must include those of the others, so that this end must be the good for man." Political philosophers are thus like "archers who have a mark to aim at . . . to hit upon what is

right" (1094a). For ancient thinkers a political order resembled an architectural construction in which the highest good, embraced by the gov-
erning body, radiated from above and gave legitimacy to subordinate
goods, which in turn functioned as criteria of choice in smaller domains
of political life.

Since the beginning, however, it became clear that this criterion was
highly controversial. Plato's *Republic* is regarded by many as a demon-
stration of the monstrosities to which the concept of the highest goods
leads in politics. The author himself, let us note, was aware that the translation of this philosophical concept into practical terms necessarily entails
the brutal violation of the existing social fabric and may be rejected by
people as a dangerous fantasy that contradicts the most basic political experience. Thus, the moment the category of the highest political good was
introduced, philosophers began to point out the complexities of the issue
and to analyze the means by which governments and theorists could min-
imize the dangers of a thoughtless, premature, or simply false conception
of the basic political criterion. Plato and Aristotle believed not only that
the absence of any moral purpose in politics was catastrophic; they also
realized the gravity of the danger that resulted from the imposition either
of an erroneous criterion or of a theoretically sound one that was inevitably bound to become perverted as soon as imperfect rulers faced the
insoluble dilemmas of imperfect societies.

To some extent one might write the whole history of Western political
philosophy as a series of attempts to grapple precisely with these problems: how to define the basic criterion of political choices and what safe-
guards to introduce in order to neutralize the inherent oppressiveness of
this criterion; how to make it more flexible, more human, closer to the true
experience of politics, so that it helps people make correct and beneficial
choices rather than stifling their initiative and becoming the source of repression and misery. Some theorists argued that the criterion should come
from nature, which would give it the status of infallibility; others maintained that, on the contrary, it should be a matter of convention, so that
people could easily adapt it to what they think are their genuine needs.
Some said the criterion ought to be as general and as abstract as possible,
not giving any privilege to a particular individual, group, or interest; others took the opposite position and maintained that it should be concrete,
derived from the actual traditions of a community or a nation and expressing its unique spirit. Some thought that those best qualified to formulate the criterion were the wise and virtuous few who should play the
role of a spiritual and moral aristocracy; others held the opinion that the
best, though not perfect, judge is the majority of citizens, and therefore
opted for democracy. Some philosophers believed in unchanged patterns
of human nature like a sense of utility, others considered spontaneous

evolution to be the ultimate arbiter. The list may continue, and probably it will continue as new hypotheses are created.

LIBERAL UTOPIANISM

Let us now examine more closely one item from this list. It differs from the others in one important respect. It comes as close as one can imagine to the belief that the unpleasant side of political choice can be reduced to a minimum; in fact, it almost negates the banal premise about the inevitability of painful choices with which I began and which I said had stimulated the first reflections on the nature of a political order. In short, it is a claim that one can construct or at least envisage a system in which people will not be forced to choose what they do not like, because there will always be goods and ideals suited to their individual aspirations. This ideal presupposes a world of plenty where no sacrifices are necessary and no frustrations await the people living in it.

The theory which gave birth to this political vision emerged from the liberal tradition and specifically from its assumption that the individual has absolute primacy vis-à-vis the group. Most of the liberals rejected the Platonic and Aristotelian notion that a legislator-philosopher should attempt to determine (or reveal) an ethical purpose different from and superior to individual moral goals. If there is any general ethical purpose in the polity, they argued, it should arise from individual choices rather than supersede them. In some theories it amounted to saying that an individual sense of happiness or pain (called "utility") is the ultimate and irreducible standard of the legitimacy of a political order. The theory I discuss is the extreme version of this argument: It claims that not only are individuals the only judges but also the sole legitimate creators of ethical and political criteria; in building institutions in a society we should therefore consciously eliminate what since Plato and Aristotle was the very nature of politics—the constant search for a compromise between the good of the individual and the good of the republic. There are conditions, it is claimed, in which this compromise is no longer needed.

To exemplify this image of a human order one can quote a passage from Robert Nozick's well-known book *Anarchy, State, and Utopia* in which he gives "the framework for utopia"; this framework

> will consist of utopias, of many different and divergent communities in which people lead different kinds of lives under different institutions. Some kinds of communities will be more attractive to most than others; communities will wax and wane. People will leave some for others or spend their whole lives in one. Utopia is . . . a place where people are at liberty to join

together voluntarily to pursue and attempt to realize their own vision of the good life in the ideal community but where no one can impose his own utopian vision upon others. . . . If the ideas must actually be tried out, there must be many communities trying out different patterns. The filtering process, the process of eliminating communities, that our framework involves is very simple: people try out living in various communities, and they leave or slightly modify the ones they don't like (find defective). Some communities will be abandoned, others will struggle along, others will split, others will flourish, gain members, and be duplicated elsewhere. Each community must win and hold the voluntary adherence of its members. No pattern is imposed on everyone, and the result will be one pattern if and only if everyone voluntarily chooses to live in accordance with that pattern of community. . . . If a person finds the character of a particular community uncongenial, he needn't choose to live in it. This is all well and good for an individual deciding which community to enter.

In the conclusion of his book Nozick emphasizes that this "model . . . designed to let you choose what you will" is not a pure fantasy. The framework for utopia is, as he says, "equivalent to the minimal state," that is, equivalent to the order which emerged not from the visionary imagination of a utopian dreamer but from rigorous philosophical reasoning. The minimal state is for him the "morally favored state, the only morally legitimate state, the only morally tolerable one." Calling it a utopia does not mean diminishing its practical or explanatory value. It is rather to give it "luster . . . to thrill the heart or inspire people to struggle or sacrifice . . . to man barricades under its banner." It simply happens that this morally favored state "is the one that best realizes the utopian aspirations of untold dreamers and visionaries. It preserves what we all can keep from the utopian tradition and opens the rest of that tradition to our individual aspirations. . . . Is not the minimal state, the framework for utopia, an inspiring vision?"

This picture of a world which is spacious enough to enclose as many ideals, communities, and ways of existence as possible is built on the assumption that no single criterion, in fact, no finite set of ethical criteria can do justice to the multiplicity of human aspirations; therefore, the only possible solution is to make the world open to all criteria and to reject every political or spiritual authority that would usurp the right to promote or disqualify some human ideals, and thus restrict the alternatives from which individuals can choose. This world can be compared to a big department store where all possible goods are available, and where people are not forced to buy only those that are currently fashionable or recommended by some authoritative agency. There is no ethical hierarchy that would tell the producers what to produce and the customers what to purchase. This department store stocks goods for hedonists and spiritualists, for Jews and Muslims, for illiterate pleasure-seekers and for refined intellectuals; there is pornography and the Bible, Plato and Stalin, communism and laissez-faire. No group or individual is deprived of the opportunity to find what they look for. Muslims are not coerced to accept the Christian faith, homosexuals are not forced to marry the other sex, monks are not distracted from the search for the absolute, and usurers are not constantly reminded about the Sermon on the Mount.

That the department store metaphor accurately renders the essence of this theory we can see from many scattered remarks in the writings of Milton Friedman. He calls the system he favors capitalism, but in fact this notion denotes something more similar to Nozick's framework for utopia than the world of Adam Smith or F. A. Hayek. The basic fact about Friedman's capitalism is its inherent diversity and openness. It not only has those properties; it also maximizes them. The development of capitalism is a constant process of making space for more goods and ideas. Friedman makes it clear that it is not a system ruled by what some have called "the capitalist ethic." Such an ethical legitimation would necessarily limit the openness of the system and make it less diversified. In other words, to impose the capitalist ethic on a society would resemble the Platonic-Aristotelian procedure of establishing a general moral criterion for a political order—obviously a criterion far less rigorous, more flexible, and more compatible with the variety of human experience than the one postulated by the Greek thinkers, but nevertheless a criterion which in the last instance is arbitrary and therefore repressive. Capitalism should not be a system where only those who accept the austere capitalist ethic can find satisfaction; it must also be a home for those who may subscribe to other ethics and who have been traditionally regarded as aliens from the point of view of the dominant ideologies: for Jews, homosexuals, eccentrics, etc. Friedman even believes that minorities who fear discrimination should, in their own interests, support capitalism because it is the only system in which they are not prevented from pursuing their unique goals.

Friedman's vision of the best order is close to Nozick's minimal state. His philosophy is deeply antistatist, anti-authoritarian, anti-absolutist. The concept of a minimal state means in practice the virtual abolition of the state, except for some of its simple protective functions. The main current of life thus flows outside politics, contrary to the Platonic-Aristotelian theory, according to which almost everything was political, that is, concerned with the well-being of the *polis*. The rejection of politics makes it possible, Friedman believes, to reduce the element of coercion inherent in every organization, especially in the state. The political procedures of selecting some goals or methods necessarily imply that those who want to make a different choice have no other option but to surrender to the dominant political power or, at best, to seek a compromise with the will of the majority. In either case their freedom of choice is considerably limited. But when political methods are replaced by the mechanisms of capitalism, and when communities adopt the arrangements of a big department store, there is no longer any need for using coercive measures. The diversity produced by these arrangements eliminates any need for the unpleasant logic of political trade-offs. As Friedman himself says, such a system "permits wide diversity. It is, in political terms, a system of proportional representation. Each man can vote, as it were, for the color of tie he wants and get it; he does not have to see what color the majority wants, and then, if he is in the minority, submit." In another passage he writes, "If I do not like what my local community does, be it in sewage disposal, or zoning, or schools. I can move to another local community. . . . If I do not like what my state does, I can move to another. If I do not like what Washington imposes, I have few alternatives in this world of jealous nations."

LIBERTARIANS AND ANARCHISTS

One may note that this richness of choices available in a liberal society was first observed in antiquity by Plato, who compared democracy to a "garment of many colors, embroidered with all kinds of hues . . . decked and diversified with every type of character" (*Rep.* 557c). Plato sounds almost Nozickian when he calls this system "a bazaar of constitutions" (557d) from which individuals can choose the constitution that they see as the most suitable for their unique preferences. In the modern age this image of the ideal society has close affinities with the vision of the social order propagated by anarchists and some socialists of anarchist persuasion. In *The German Ideology* the young Marx craved a system in which one could be a hunter in the morning, a fisherman in the afternoon, a shepherd in the evening, and a literary critic at night. The mature Marx had few moments of anarchistic weakness; the most notable one comes from the well-known passage in the *Critique of the Gotha Program* which predicts that future society "will be able to inscribe on its banners: from each according to his abilities, to each according to his needs." Prince Kropotkin's *Modern Science and Anarchism* gives the following description of the social ideal:

> The anarchists conceive a society in which all the mutual relations of its members are regulated, not by laws, not by authorities, whether self-imposed or elected, but by mutual agreements between the members of that society, and by a sum of social customs and habits—not petrified by law, routine, or superstition, but continually developing and continually readjusted,

in accordance with the ever-growing requirements of a free life, stimulated by the progress of science, invention, and the steady growth of higher ideals. No ruling authorities, then. No government of man by man; no crystallization and immobility, but a continual evolution—such as we see in Nature.

Of modern visions, E. P. Thompson's "Open Letter to Leszek Kolakowski" (published in *The Socialist Register* in 1973) provides a perfect sample:

> With sources of power easily available, some men and women might choose to live in unified communities, sited, like Cistercian monasteries, in centres of great natural beauty, where agricultural, industrial and intellectual pursuits might be combined. Others might prefer the variety and pace of an urban life which rediscovers some of the qualities of the city-state. Others will prefer a life of seclusion, and many will pass between all three. Scholars would follow the disputes of different schools, in Paris, Jakarta, or Bogota.

Nozick and Friedman were of course aware of these anarchistic affinities. In a *Playboy* interview Friedman admitted this explicitly by wishing anarchists good luck and praising them for pointing in the right direction. Nozick and Friedman on the one hand and the anarchists on the other had a common and, one has to admit, correct presupposition. All of them rightly believed that a world of increasing diversity has fewer problems that have to be settled through the process of negotiations, whereas in a world of scarcity very many difficult and always unsatisfactory decisions have to be made that are likely to look arbitrary and frustrating to the parties involved. Plato and Aristotle's *polis* was undoubtedly a world of scarcity where the rules of distribution seemed essential; under modern capitalism, on the other hand, despite its remoteness from the ideal of maximum diversity, no such urgent political procedures are needed. Whoever has visited both Macy's and any of the state-run shops of Eastern Europe will not challenge the evident message of the libertarian theory.

The difference between modern American minimal-state theorists and anarchists is, however, no less significant than the similarity. Friedman and Nozick admire the economic system which for Kropotkin, Marx, and others was a synonym of wickedness. For the American libertarians maintain that theory and history show capitalism to be the only system capable of producing a high degree of diversity. What for anarchists was an obscure vision of the future order, for the libertarians is a matter of hard facts. They accordingly regard anarchists as either impotent to realize their ideal, or misled in thinking that their goals can be achieved through socialist means, or simply stupid in rejecting the capitalist institutions that are said to be the only mechanisms which can at least partly make their dream a reality.

DIVIDED LOYALTIES

Having said that libertarianism is undeniably an effective way to mini-
mize the hardships of choice and to neutralize the repressiveness of political criteria, I do not wish to imply that the libertarian solution is perfect.
A lot has been said against it, and at least a part of the critique has some
validity. Let me analyze the objection I consider most important.

An inhabitant of the libertarian world of plenty has two loyalties—one
which ties him to his own community, and the other which makes him a
supporter of diversity as a general principle of the whole society. He must
be both a person of a specific culture—a Jew, a Muslim, a Catholic, a European, a communist, etc.—and a dedicated adherent of the multicultural
creed. He must be both closed within a certain cultural tradition and open
to, as well as tolerant of, all traditions.

"Is such a combination possible?" one might ask. "Why not?" seems
the obvious answer. After all, most of us are to some extent the living
examples of such a combination. Each of us has both larger and narrower loyalties, and this, I presume, need not be a source of intellectual
or moral schizophrenia. A conference or a debating club might be thus
regarded as a prototype of a good society where Muslims, Christians,
communists, and atheists exchange arguments and look critically at
each other's as well as their own points of view. To some degree such a
model was considered by the classical liberals, for example by John Stuart Mill, as a miniature of a healthy social order. If the critical mind is
the main creative force of civilization, then nothing is more natural than
a state of different loyalties which generates a constant need to test
ideas, introduce new ones, compare them with the old ones, etc. The
classical liberals believed in the evolution of social wisdom, hoping that
a permanent clash among different points of view would lead to a sort
of cultural miscegenation—the best remedy against short-sighted
parochialism.

Whether these hopes were justified need not concern us here. What is
important is that this doctrine of society as debating club has little to do
with Nozick's utopia and Friedman's capitalism. The libertarian vision of
a society where there was enough safe space for every creed and occupation was inconceivable to the classical liberals; they did not want to offer
shelters to small groups and eccentric ideologies. They rather encouraged
those groups and the representatives of those ideologies to subvert retro-
grade aspects of the traditional beliefs and institutions. Diversity was not
for them a state of non-interference but rather a vehicle for generating
more conflicts, as a result of which new structures were to replace the old
ones and a new consensus was to emerge on the ruins of old philosophies
and social stereotypes.

Yet the creative role of omnipresent conflicts was not thought to produce a divergence of allegiances. A liberal did not have two different loyalties—one to his group, and the other to mankind; he rather tended to identify them with each other. Every new force of dissenters—women, slaves, the oppressed nationalities—fighting against the old authority was believed to represent mankind, to carry out the fight in the name of the human race, and in the long run to open new vistas for all human minds. Allegiance to the women's cause was thus for John Stuart Mill indistinguishable from allegiance to the cause of progress, that is, to the cause of people at large. The logic of the debating club required that women and other oppressed groups be given a voice, but it was also expected that their voice change the general substance and form of discourse within a society. This identification of narrower and larger loyalties, which legitimized every form of dissent as a contribution to the dynamics of progress, implied a certain conception of culture. Liberals thought of culture in terms of hierarchy; to some extent they may be said to have inverted the traditional hierarchy of conservatives. The process of evolution was to indicate which parts of social structures were anachronistic—these were put on the lower level—and which parts contained the seeds of the future and deserved a place in the higher reaches of the cultural hierarchy. Thus, heresies became preferable to orthodoxies, dissidents to mainstream thinkers, minorities to majorities, atheists to fideists. Abolishing the throne-and-altar alliance and building democracy had not brought about harmonious equality within communities. New forces of oppression and authority emerged which broke the egalitarian principles on which democracy was founded; therefore, dissenters were expected to undermine democratic tyranny and to take in their hands the cause of the liberty of mankind.

The modern libertarians are not as lucky as the nineteenth-century liberals were on the question of allegiance. True, they pay little attention to this question, but one glance at their theory suffices to show that the libertarians' world does not permit an identification of dissent and loyalty. The first loyalty that binds an individual to Nozick's utopia and Friedman's capitalism stems from the acceptance of the principle of equality. Not only are all communities equal—in the sense that no moral, intellectual, or political authority can impose the criteria of choice on them (this, of course, has nothing to do with material equality)—but there should not be any conflict among them, because this would amount to interference in their internal order. The whole point of the system of diversity is to make powerless all such interference and to enable every individual to find a secure place. Nozick's and Friedman's worlds contain no victors in the competition of ideas, for their systems were conceived in such a way as to preclude victory. There are, to use Friedman's example, no authoritatively good ties or bad ties, and discussions leading to compromises on this or on many other issues are not needed. All those who are dissatisfied with the available choices can found a new community, equal to other communities, or hope that spontaneous development will one day produce a community compatible with their unique preferences.

This does not mean, however, that the libertarians' world is entirely value-free and contains absolutely no presuppositions. The most obvious and important ones—the sacredness of private property and negative freedom—have been taken over from the doctrine of classical liberalism. This implies a form of ethical discrimination, that is, the rejection of systems that do not recognize private property and that promote a moral purpose that requires curtailing individual freedom. Logically speaking, this should entail a very strong ethical position. In assuming the sacredness of private property and the autonomy of the individual one not only opposes alternative moral hierarchies (for example, a socialist one) but also presumably defends a particular hierarchy in which the primary goods of private property and the autonomous individual coexist and are coordinated with other goods, generating a large and complex ethical system. One would also have to accept certain social (cultural) norms and historically internalized forms of behavior that secure the functioning of this system in a society. Such attitudes are, roughly speaking, characteristic of modern neoconservatives; they are not, however, typical of libertarians, at least not of those who subscribe to the idea of diversity as an organizing principle. Because they equate private property with the autonomy of the individual, libertarians refrain from entering into arguments in which the value of private property might be regarded as one of many competing values. They are rather inclined to think that they have been able to overcome the seemingly inconclusive controversies between competing values by letting individuals *choose their own*. Once we accept—their argument runs—the sacredness of private property and the autonomy of the individual, we will have opened the door to the realization of other values, even those which have been traditionally inimical to the liberal hierarchy; the opposite is not true. As Milton Friedman wrote in *Free to Choose*: "A society that puts equality . . . ahead of freedom will end up with neither equality nor freedom. . . . On the other hand, a society that puts freedom first will, as a happy by-product, end up with both greater freedom and greater equality." The same holds not only for equality, but also for other values.

Strictly speaking, this is not a position of cultural relativism. Libertarians do not say that libertarianism is as good as authoritarianism; they do not even say that communism is as arbitrary as democracy or that a Christian ethics as much a matter of taste as a lesbian ethic. What they imply, however, is that non-libertarians will be better off once they accept the primary libertarian values as a basis for the general institutional framework. This acceptance—the libertarians claim—will not force those who hold other views to make any significant doctrinal sacrifices. Communism may be morally repulsive and politically dangerous, but a communist enclave might very well exist within the Great Society which will harbor similar enclaves for other non-libertarian groups, all respecting the overall framework. Cultural relativism, or rather cultural blindness, becomes thus a likely consequence of the Great Society. To give an example: A communist may be lured to enter the libertarian order by the promise that he will not have to renounce his views, but he will believe this only so long as he is convinced that the libertarian values on which the minimal state is grounded will not infringe on his doctrine. If there is a possibility that the values of the Great Society itself can be organically integrated into a specific culture within it, the communist will certainly decline an offer to join the Great Society; he will fear justifiably that the general institutional framework might be used by that specific, libertarian culture against him and against other groups; he must be sure that all groups and communities, like his own, are considered equally neutral from the point of view of the ruling libertarian values. Cultural relativism, though not a necessary theoretical assumption for libertarians, must eventually emerge as an actual practice in the libertarian order. Without it, one would have to distinguish between groups that can and those that cannot enter the Great Society, according to whether or not they accept the sacredness of private property, the autonomy of the individual, and the consequences of those values. This is of course a perfectly valid procedure (which goes back to Plato and Aristotle and is supported today, among others, by neoconservatives), but it virtually destroys the claim of diversity that was initially attached to the Great Society, the libertarian framework for, or department store of, utopias.

The second loyalty that would survive the establishment of libertarianism links an individual with a community: ethnic, religious, professional, etc., each of these being naturally hierarchical. A Catholic, a Muslim, a Jew, a homosexual, a feminist, all of them by joining or being born into one of those communities have a right to accept various types of hierarchy and various types of authority. This naturally follows from the nature of the Great Society. But every culture is animated by its own truth; therefore every group finds its own raison d'être in promoting the ethical system it sees as true and morally binding. That was precisely the reason why these groups decided to join the libertarian order: They accepted its rules in order to gain more freedom to develop their culture. There might of course be disagreements among the members of a community, but those disagreements concern the modification of hierarchy; they do not and cannot aim at the abolition of all authority or hierarchy, unless one's purpose is the annihilation of the community whose values one joined the Great Society to develop—except for the community of individualist relativists.

A libertarian thus faces the following dilemma: He accepts the equality of the truths and value systems of all communities within the Great Society; at the same time, he accepts a certain moral hierarchy of his own community. He is thus divided between two beliefs: one which compels him to behave as if all norms were relative and it would be improper as well as dangerous to strive for a universal truth; and another which makes him an adherent of a definite set of ideas considered truer and better than the ideas propagated by other communities. On the one hand, he finds, to use Nozick's expression, "an inspiring vision" in the cause of culture blindness and thinks he should "man barricades" to spread this gospel; on the other hand, he chooses a certain culture together with its built-in mechanism of moral and intellectual discrimination against other cultures.

THE RETURN OF PLATO

Which of these two loyalties is stronger? How is the conflict between them usually resolved? Which of these beliefs tends to dominate the other?

The classical answer to these questions can be found in Plato's analysis of the pluralistic society, which, as we remember, he compared to "the garment of many colours." This is how Plato describes a libertarian man:

> He does not accept or admit into the guardhouse the words of truth when anyone tells him that some pleasures arise from honorable and good desires, and others from those that are base, and that we ought to practice and esteem the one and control and subdue the others, but he shakes his head at all such admonitions and avers that they are all alike and to be equally esteemed. . . . He also live[s] out his life in this fashion, day by day indulging the appetite of the day, now winebibbing and abandoning himself to the lascivious pleasing of the flute and again drinking only water and dieting, and at one time exercising his body, and sometimes idling and neglecting all things, and at another time seeming to occupy himself with philosophy. And frequently he goes in for politics and bounces up and says and does whatever enters his head. And if military men excite his emulation, thither he rushes, and if moneyed men, to that he turns, and there is no order or compulsion in his existence, but he calls this life of his the life of pleasure and freedom and happiness and cleaves to it to the end. . . .
> [He is] a devotee of equality. . . . He is a manifold man stuffed with most excellent differences, and like that city he is the fair and many-coloured one

whom many a man and woman would count fortunate in his life, as containing within himself the greatest number of patterns of constitutions and
qualities. (*Rep.* 561b-e)

Plato seems to maintain that of the two beliefs we described previously,
the first one is the stronger and will eventually eliminate the second. An
individual living in a libertarian society will soon lose his devotion to the
Jewish, Catholic, or Protestant morality and will cease to believe one to be
truer than another. Like many different colors, all creeds and philosophies
will look equal to him, that is, equally attractive, but at the same time
equally arbitrary. He could indeed realize the anarchists' dream and become a religious poet in the morning, an atheist philosopher in the afternoon, a thrifty bourgeois in the evening; but in fact, this is possible only
because he is none of these and has no genuine understanding or love for
any definite cultural preferences.

Plato seems to say something more. He implies that the triumph of the
libertarian-egalitarian mentality over all cultural hierarchies is possible
only because this mentality is totally devoid of any meaning. It is the triumph of the power of nihilism in the most elementary sense of the word.
The "inspiring vision" of the libertarian utopia turns out to be, on closer
examination, the luster of the flicker denoting no philosophical or any
other truth. It is the illustration of intellectual entropy. To nineteenth-
century thinkers the liberal mind appeared a product of evolution and the
culmination of the growing rationality of mankind. By contrast, the libertarian mind, as Plato sees it, resembles the product of a disintegration
which has gradually stripped it of every conviction, in fact, of any adherence to the category of truth.

Justifying the relevance of Plato's diagnosis to the cult of diversity in
liberal societies is not difficult. One can find Plato's followers, like Allan
Bloom, who repeat the Athenian philosopher's argument almost verba-
tim. One can also find philosophers, like Alasdair MacIntyre, who on the
basis of the Aristotelian-Thomistic tradition try to combat the modern notion of the equality of cultures and to rescue the value of hierarchy. It is
even easier to find instances of the libertarian malaise in the popular idiom; such examples pervade the whole range of political output, from the
dissertations of respectable scholars to the manifestos of American ideologues. One would be tempted to cite endless cases of the use of that favorite term in modern political jargon—"culture"—to which almost
everyone feels obliged to give lip service but which today means almost
exclusively something repressive and dangerously autocratic, or something entirely harmless in its subjectivity, like fashion. In both cases it is
assumed that under no condition should one draw more general conclusions and attempt to give a universal meaning to any specific culture. It is

surprising that the modern prophets of diversity, who never tire of speaking of whites, blacks, Europeans, non-Europeans, men, and as cultural entities, prohibit any dialogue about the comparative value or cultural hierarchy which specific members of these groups—e.g., Jews, Muslims, Confucians, Christians, liberals, conservatives—contribute to the common heritage of mankind; this would amount to racism, or sexism, or cultural imperialism.

Plato would have been proud of his accurate predictions if he could see that in the current ideological climate the only conflict that arouses emotion is the one about the equality of cultures. But if all cultures offer equally valid contributions, and if an individual is prohibited from evaluating a political order in terms of a more universal cultural hierarchy, then one should conclude that from the point of view of this order the values of the constituent cultures are worthless. And if the Culture (capital C) of the whole libertarian order consists of valueless cultures (small c), then the overarching Culture itself is valueless. The garment of many colors looks colorless.

Let us make our task more difficult. Let us look at the argument of someone who is not a doctrinaire libertarian but a serious and responsible thinker, and see if there, too, the Platonic argument is applicable. I am thinking of the British liberal-conservative philosopher John Gray, who openly distances himself from the nihilistic presuppositions of unlimited openness. In his Latham Memorial Lecture (a revised version of which appears in *The Salisbury Review* of September 1988) he defended the basic point of the diversity thesis. In modern societies, he said, there is no "moral solidarity"; the existing differences of cultures make it impossible and the striving for it dangerous. But he did not accept the Friedmanian and Nozickian thesis that the cure for diversity is more diversity and that the imperfections of the hitherto-existing criteria of social choice will disappear when there are no criteria at all. His solution is instead that "we may yet be able to draw on the resource of another kind of solidarity— that of civilised men and women, practitioners of different traditions, who nevertheless have in common a perception of enmity in regard to the totalitarian states and re-barbarising movements of our time."

I believe Gray's view does not invalidate Plato's argument that the Culture of equal cultures is empty. Gray seems to say that it is empty only in the sense that it does not contain any moral consensus. He emphasizes however that it is not empty in another very important respect. It is based, he claims, on civilizational consensus. Gray's position is debatable on various counts. In the first place, he unnecessarily assents to the thesis that Western civilization lacks a common moral bond and that therefore it is hopeless to argue about what constitutes its core. This thesis, popular among the intolerant preachers of diversity, must logically lead to cultural relativism; I do not see how, given the premise, such a consequence can be avoided. But Gray is not a cultural relativist because he makes a distinction between those who belong to the civilization and the barbarians who threaten it. One wonders, however, what may account for the difference between "moral solidarity," which is said to be absent in the modern world, and "the solidarity of civilized men and women," which is believed to exist and to distinguish those men and women from barbarians. How can a civilizational consensus be maintained without any reference to morality; and if it can, how can it not be empty? I do not think the difference can be substantiated unless by civilizational solidarity one means the habits of civilized behavior, which make possible the harmonious coexistence of various cultures. But then one may ask if these habits, important as they are, constitute a sufficient ground for distinguishing "civilised men and women" from barbarians?

Gray's argument is more resolute: If we, as people of different cultures, cannot agree on positive norms, we can at least agree on negative ones—on what we reject as inimical to civilization. He mentions two forces which can unite us in this manner—the totalitarian states and the re-barbarizing movements of our time. As regards the first enemy, the history of the last seven decades has witnessed remarkably generous support for those states (including some indirect support from libertarian foreign-policy "non-interventionists"). The disappearance of totalitarianism that we observe today, but which was long ago and quite prematurely buried by the distinguished intellects of Western civilization, makes things more complicated. There will certainly be many offspring of totalitarianism which will be even more difficult to identify so as to form a civilizational consensus in response. We face the same difficulty with the re-barbarizing movements of our time. On the basis of other statements by John Gray, I can fathom the danger he has in mind, and I might add I wholeheartedly agree with his diagnosis. But most of those movements act under the banner of cultural diversity, and I do not see how we can arrive at "a common perception of enmity" that would permit us to condemn them as neo-barbarians.

Gray's argument is not convincing: Either "the solidarity of civilized men and women" is different from "moral solidarity," in which case it is empty or superficial and thus subject to Plato's argument; or this solidarity is not empty, in which case it contains moral criteria. In the latter case, we are back to the problem of the criterion of choice, which is close to abandoning the idea of diversity as an organizing principle.

Let me conclude. The aim of this essay is not to argue against diversity, but rather against the claim that increasing diversity eliminates the problem of choice and the need to argue about the moral purpose of a political order. The price that has to be paid for the illusion that this claim can be realized is higher than the cost of a constant and inconclusive search for the standards of right and wrong which political orders are meant to serve. One must reject the dichotomy of a totalitarian dictatorship, theocratic and ideological, or a libertarian minimal state, morally and culturally sterile—a gigantic prison or a gigantic department store. Plato's republic would definitely be an unpleasant place to live. But is its absolute opposite the best regime a rational human being can think of? Who would like to spend one's entire life in a shopping mall?

NOTE

"Society as a Department Store," by Ryszard Legutko, first appeared in *Critical Review* 4, no. 3 (1990): 327–43. Reprinted by permission.

2

+

The Trouble with Toleration

There is something sacrosanct about toleration in modern political folklore: Without much exaggeration, it can be said that the triumph of liberalism has elevated this category into the ultimate and almost the only generally acceptable litmus test of morality. At the very least, no other single category—not justice, not equality, not even freedom—has won such wide moral support in the Western world. What the radical philosopher Robert Paul Wolff wrote almost thirty years ago would probably arouse little controversy today: Just as the basic value of a monarchy is loyalty and that of a military dictatorship is honor, so the basic value of the modern pluralist democracy is tolerance. The common wisdom permeating modern political theory has it that one can get away with anything as long as one is tolerant. Intolerance is more to be feared than all traditional sins. Human vices are deplorable, yet within the framework of toleration they can be tamed and civilized. When this framework is missing, it is believed that our social and political life suffer from mortal disease.

Not surprisingly, the question of whether the concept of toleration deserves such high esteem is rarely taken up today, although the limits of toleration are recognized and few thinkers or politicians would profess a doctrine of absolute toleration, a concept hardly defensible to any non-doctrinaire mind. Yet whenever conflict arises and a new idea or movement challenges the status quo, a call for toleration usually outweighs any demand that such an idea or movement should justify its dissenting position. In fact, to make such a demand is frequently interpreted precisely as an expression of intolerance. Most of those who write about or defend toleration ignore the cost, primarily intellectual and moral, of the puzzling omnipotence which has been given to a category that originally occupied a far more modest position. Logically, it would seem that since the contemporary Western world is much more humane—"tolerant," one might say—than Europe of the seventeenth and eighteenth centuries, there should be less need to talk about toleration. What has occurred within our philosophical and moral outlook to keep us preoccupied with a concept that we apparently have been very successful in implementing? Stalin once said that the closer the socialist paradise, the more numerous and more powerful its enemies. Can it be that a similar fear haunts the modern liberal conscience?

In the classical formulations of toleration, those of Bayle, Locke, and Voltaire, the first problem one stumbles upon is to what extent toleration has a distinct meaning of its own and to what extent it can be reduced to other notions. Voltaire's *Traité sur la tolérance*, for example, was occasioned by the unjust sentencing to death of Jean Calas, a French Protestant accused of killing his own Catholic son. One wonders to what degree the famous *philosophe* was entitled to speak of toleration in this context. Is justice, fairness, the rule of law not enough to prevent similar cases from happening again? Will our judicial system work better if to good laws, good legal institutions, and good judges we add "toleration"? Was Jean Calas sentenced to death because the judiciary system in France did not function properly and because the French did not respect the elementary requirements of justice, or did he die because the French Catholics lacked tolerance?

One reason these and similar doubts arise is that the intolerance, the opposite of toleration, of which Bayle, Locke, and Voltaire spoke was most often identified with violence of the most brutal kind, as in Locke's "persecute, torment, destroy, and kill other men upon pretence of religion." It is even more strongly illustrated by Voltaire, who wrote of Irish Catholics

sacrificing, as an acceptable offering, the lives of their Protestant brethren, by burying them alive, hanging up mothers upon gibbets, and tying their daughters round their necks to see them expire together; ripping up women with child, taking the half-formed infant from the womb, and throwing it to swine or dogs to be devoured; putting a dagger into the hands of their manacled prisoners and forcing them to plunge it into the breasts of their fathers, their mothers, their wives, or children, thereby hoping to make them guilty of parricide, and damn their souls while they destroyed their bodies.

The consequence of identifying intolerance with violence, persecution, and cruelty was the conviction that anything lessening the risk of violence, persecution, and cruelty counted as toleration. Thus a call for toleration was, in Locke's *Letter Concerning Toleration*, a call for "charity," "faith which works . . . by love," "meekness," "good-will." To these could be added other virtues and rules of behavior to make people's interactions more harmonious: good manners, a sense of justice, tact, knowledge, honesty, respect for others, open-mindedness. It was also asserted that toleration was linked to self-preservation and self-interest: the first manifesting itself in the need for social peace rather than civil wars to which anyone could fall victim; the second in the beneficent connection between toleration and trade, which soon became evident to many observers of social life. Yet not only virtues and natural dispositions contributed to neutralizing intolerance and building toleration; various vices could also serve the aim. For instance, hypocrisy, one of those undoubtedly and often condemned human frailties, nevertheless could be useful. Voltaire's treatise gives us a telling anecdote about a Dominican and a Jesuit who had fiercely quarrelled:

> The mandarin being informed of this scandalous behavior ordered them both to be sent to prison. A submandarin asked His Excellency how long he would please to have them remain in confinement. Until they are both agreed, said the judge. Then, my lord, answered the submandarin, they will remain in prison all their days. Well, then, said the mandarin. Let them stay until they forgive one another. That they will never do rejoined the deputy; I know them very well. Indeed, said the mandarin; then let it be until they appear to do so.

The scope given to the concept of toleration in the classics is intriguing. Is there anything specific in toleration that distinguishes it from other apparently related but far more tangible notions and phenomena like kindness or disinterestedness? What will be left of toleration if we deprive it of tact and justice, of love and meekness, of charity and good manners, of knowledge and curiosity, of instincts for self-interest and self-preservation, of hypocrisy and other private vices which are public virtues? If we possess most of these qualities, is it necessary to invoke the concept of toleration? What would be gained?

One plausible answer is that toleration, whatever its precise meaning, is attached to all these virtues, vices, instincts, and habits. Without them, or in opposition to them, or abstracted from them and treated separately as an autonomous quality, toleration is empty and meaningless. Possibly, there is nothing conceptually faulty with insistently relating toleration to other practices of moral behavior; pure toleration, distilled of all related notions, may be of dubious worth and—if separated from related practices—even harmful. Advocating toleration without love, justice, rule of law, self-interest, hypocrisy, and so on may be like advocating courage without the training of character, at best an arid exercise in philosophical speculation and at worst a form of subversion aimed at the most vital and widely shared values of social life. Therefore, such "pure" toleration might well bring results hardly compatible with the ordinary sense of the concept. A tolerant individual could thus be either someone who lives peacefully with his philosophical and religious adversaries, or someone who antagonizes people by ordering them to obey an abstract rule, which he claims will bring peace and harmony to all, unrelated to experience. In the first case, tolerance is a virtue of an individual human character; in the second, a principle to which human habit should conform.

Voltaire himself perfectly illustrated both of these attitudes. There were in fact two Voltaires: the first is the author of *Traité sur la tolérance*, a good Christian (at least pretending to be one), defending toleration as the culmination of many moral components. The other is the Voltaire of *écrasez l'infâme*, the visionary of the Enlightenment who sought to elevate toleration on the ruins of Christianity, the extirpation of which he regarded as the major mission of his life. In his struggle against *l'infâme*, Voltaire committed precisely the error that the idea of toleration was meant to prevent. He fell victim to intellectual hubris: Armed with his philosophical humanism, he set out to eradicate the evil and falsehood that people, because of the inertia of tradition and ignorance, still allegedly harbored in themselves.

John Locke was more cautious. His *Letter* spelled out a case for toleration that was based on an attitude of humility toward truth. To generalize his insight, one can say that if there is some specificity in the idea of toleration, irreducible to other ideas and habits, it reveals itself in the acceptance of human imperfection; it expresses the effort to put into practice the ultimate moral standards—truth being the most vital one. Locke formulated his argument against the magistrates who claimed the power to punish the false religion and to defend the true one. We need toleration, he argued, when we do not have the knowledge or certainty of what is true, or when the nature of controversy is such that it precludes the establishment of any common ground. The latter case clearly applies to religious conflicts which, as Locke repeatedly emphasized, are to a considerable degree a matter of faith and cannot be settled through rational argument. The purpose of toleration was to draw the attention of all parties involved to the danger of arrogant and hasty transformation of true or seemingly true concepts into political instruments.

Such a rendering of toleration was clearly modest, and there was not much philosophy in it, except perhaps an implied empiricist distrust of abstract and aprioristic formulas functioning as criteria in political life. This version of toleration is often called negative: It usually limits itself to negative qualifications. Contrary to what Voltaire the prophet of the Enlightenment (in contrast to the Voltaire of *Traité*) thought, it neither indicates truth nor promotes it, nor even helps intellectually in the process of establishing truth. Toleration does not presuppose any identifiable metaphysics or ethics or political philosophy. Locke and Voltaire (in his *Treatise*), while stressing that toleration and truth are in practice related, did not say that truth as such is a repressive notion. They did not therefore suggest that in the name of toleration we should avoid or suspend truth. They did not even allow that there could be several truths of equal validity and that therefore no truth could enjoy superiority. Locke believed that his religion was the true one. Voltaire saw nothing reprehensible in the fact that some religions were dominant in certain societies and that those who belonged to these religions were given leading political positions. He thought it natural that certain government functions were thus not accessible to some people because of their religious beliefs. By modern standards this does not seem a particularly libertarian position, but it is reconcilable with the general idea of toleration. Hierarchy and intolerance are two different things. The aim of toleration is not to be a substitute for equality, justice, and other moral and political qualities. Toleration cannot make any positive claims such as that a certain category of persons should be given certain political or social positions, specifically on the grounds of toleration.

From the beginning, however, it was obvious that the advocates of toleration were tempted to transcend the narrow limits of the negative version. The temptation was to make it more committed in the struggle for a better world, more partisan, more positive. The decisive step toward a positive interpretation was to neutralize certain points of view and to promote others; to oppose those philosophies, religions, and social norms which are coercive, dominating, authoritarian, monolithic; and to support other philosophies, religions, and social norms that do not have these unpleasant characteristics. Thus, toleration would no longer be blind, uncommitted, indifferent to the final result of the dispute between contending parties. On the contrary, it would be a major actor in the dispute, strengthening one party and withdrawing its support from the other. It would consist not in refraining from doing certain things, but in acting in a certain way, in choosing and committing oneself to the cause of freedom. By being passive, by not choosing and committing oneself, one ran the risk of becoming an unwitting accomplice of the intolerant party.

The history of the last two hundred years of Western political philosophy may be interpreted, among other things, as a gradual decline of negative toleration and a simultaneous growth of its positive counterpart. Most of these efforts have aimed at no less than the discovery of the final key to the tolerant world, that is, the creation of a framework of ethical guidelines which effectively prevent intolerance. To put it differently, there has been the hope that the forces of toleration could finally achieve victory in the war against the forces of intolerance, or—even if reality proves resistant—that at least we will have a clear formula of the strategy and the general goal. This tradition extends from John Stuart Mill, who located the source of oppression in the customs and social stereotypes and thus attributed a special role to eccentrics constantly undermining our thoughtless sense of stability, to Herbert Marcuse, who came to a somewhat baffling conclusion in *A Critique of Pure Tolerance* that "liberating tolerance" meant "intolerance against movements from the Right, and toleration of movements from the Left."

During the last decade or so, another solution of the problem of how to make the world safe for toleration has come from a group of thinkers who like to label themselves as postmodern. In spite of important differences among them, they seem to share a conviction that we can, we should, and we have already begun to liquidate the intellectual basis of intolerance. Negative tolerance was defective, it is claimed, because with respect to truth it preached only humility. It is truth as such, regardless of the degree of arrogance or humility with which it is professed, that is responsible for intolerance. Whatever we regard as true, be it in philosophy, morals, ways of life, criteria of permissiveness, is always exclusive. It inevitably relegates some people outside the sphere of what is normal and respectable. For example, by stressing one's heterosexuality one may be suspected of implying that there is something objectively wrong with homosexuality, which in turn makes one susceptible to the charge of depriving homosexuals of their dignity and consequently of inciting discrimination against them.

From truth to persecution there is, then, a straight and logical transition, and the obvious implication is that in order to secure toleration we must abandon the traditional criteria of evaluation, and in more ambitious projects, we must abandon traditional metaphysics and the epistemology from which the criterion of truth derived its strength. We must eradicate once and for all the sense of philosophical certainty that permitted some to look down on others, a sense of certainty stemming from the assumption that our world has an essence or foundation reachable by the cognitive faculties of the wise, who then impose it on the ignorant. Once we annihilate the assumption of philosophical essentialism and foundationalism, the sting of intolerance will be cut off.

Truth, wrote Michel Foucault in *Power/Knowledge*, is not something to be discovered but rather "a regime": "the ensemble of rules according to which the true and the false are separated and specific effects of power attached to the true." For the old followers of the truth-as-regime theory, for Marx, Lenin, and their disciples, the power holders were explicit: the bourgeoisie, capitalists, the industrial-military complex. For the following generations of the philosophers of suspicion—for poststructuralists, postmodernists, deconstructionists—the enemy who holds truth through power is more obscure. We usually see only the effects, not the perpetrators: a frame of mind, a system of concepts, a philosophy. This power has become thus even less visible than a dictatorship of customs and opinion, so feared by nineteenth-century liberals, and more harmful to the human mind. For Derrida it would be "phallogocentrism," a domination of human consciousness and behavior by male rationalism. The cause of toleration has been given a new target, more deeply hidden than previous ones. Where once it was the Catholic Church, then political authoritarianism, then customs and prevailing opinion, now it is philosophy, language, intellectual education.

This program of liberation amounts to a virtual abolition of philosophy in the form in which it has existed for two and a half millennia. Along with the concept of truth, other basic notions and distinctions have been divested of their philosophical legitimacy and come to be viewed as the potential carriers of oppression: essence, nature, subject-object dichotomy, reason, good, evil. Until recently conceived of as "strong thinking," philosophy must be replaced by something far less demanding, less authoritarian and patronizing, in short, by Gianni Vattimo's *il pensiero debole* ("weak thinking"). What will it be like? Some call up the ancient quarrel between rhetoric, championed by the sophists, and philosophy, whose greatest defenders were Socrates, Plato, and Aristotle. They argue that we are witnessing today the decline of strong philosophy, inhumanely objective and hierarchical, and the triumph of essentially weak rhetoric: The criteria of social coexistence, adaptable and malleable, have begun to play a more important role than the suprahuman criteria of truth. As Richard Rorty put it, democracy has become prior to philosophy.

What philosophers once interpreted as a disinterested pursuit of truth has now been replaced by social praxis, by dialogue and communication, by deconstruction and hermeneutics, by play and spontaneous expression, by individual or collective therapy. The abolition of philosophy has to lead to the abolition of the distinction between the center and the periphery. In the new world there are no peripheries, or—what amounts to the same thing—there are nothing but peripheries. Some enthusiasts of "weak thinking," like G. B. Madison, do not hesitate to speak of the new era in human relations:

> The politics of postmodernity, like postmodern philosophy itself, will . . . no longer be one of opposites. Oppositional thinking goes along with metaphysical hierarchies, and it is precisely these which are being undermined by the new postmodern, global civilization now coming into being. The new era has the potential of being one not of metaphysical, essence-bound homogeneity and modernistic uniformity but of difference, particularity, plurality, and heterogeneity. In regard, for instance, to the new geo-economic order, we are witnessing the emergence of a complex, interlocking, and decentered network of institutions in which there is no longer any identifiable source, origin, or centre.

Those who live in such a world will no longer be troubled by the metaphysical horror or the specter of nothingness; on the contrary, a sense of Kundera's "lightness of being" will produce in them what Rorty has called "the air of light-minded aestheticism," an attitude which the American philosopher has openly welcomed and approved:

> The encouragement of light-mindedness about traditional philosophical topics serves the same purposes as does the encouragement of light-mindedness about traditional theological topics. Like the rise of large market economies, the increase in literacy, the proliferation of artistic genres, and the insouciant pluralism of contemporary culture, such philosophical superficiality and light-mindedness helps along the disenchantment of the world. It helps make the world's inhabitants more pragmatic, more tolerant, more liberal, more receptive to the appeal of instrumental rationality.

On a popular level, this frame of mind, as well as the hope attached to it, is illustrated by the kind of postmodernist fiction which in many cases is built on one symptomatic pattern: The protagonist (and with him the reader) is forced by circumstances or by manipulation to repeatedly reorganize his interpretation of reality and to pass through heuristic trials which reveal to him the arbitrariness of his former philosophical self-assured seriousness.

A somewhat different version of positive toleration expresses itself in an attitude rendered by one Polish author as " sympathetic openness." Since, as Goethe put it, "to tolerate is to offend," we cannot, following his indication, confine ourselves to negative toleration which others might find patronizing and humiliating. To the modern liberal British philosopher R. M. Hare, man acknowledges the ideal of toleration if he acknowledges "a readiness to respect other people's ideals as if they were his own."

Those who champion this form of toleration do not maintain—and such possible misunderstanding must be made clear—that sympathetic openness should prevail only in the initial stages of contacts with unknown individuals, groups, and opinions. It thus excludes the possibility of being sympathetically open to something as yet unknown, of then encountering it, finding it repulsive, and ultimately deciding to treat it neither with sympathy nor with openness. Rather, sympathetic openness must be present at all stages of contact with other people's opinions and ideals. Hare argues for the plausibility of his thesis and tells us how expansive the limits of liberals' respect for other points of view ought to be:

> It is part of the liberal's ideal that a good society, whatever else it is, is one in which the ideals and interests of all are given equal consideration. It is, to use Kantian language, a kingdom of ends in which all are, at least poten-

tially, legislating members. . . . He may even think that a diversity of ideals is in itself a good thing . . . because it takes all sorts to make a world. If the liberal's ideal is of any of these kinds, he is not betraying it but following it if he tolerates other people's pursuit of their ideals, provided that, where the pursuit of one ideal hinders the pursuit of another, there shall be . . . a just distribution of advantages and disadvantages. It is only the last proviso which prevents the liberal from allowing even the fanatic to pursue his ideals without impediment; but the liberal is not required by his own ideal to tolerate intolerance.

In practice, it might be difficult to be sympathetically open to all points of view. This, however, does not discredit the sympathetic attitude itself, since what matters here is not infinite sympathy to an infinite number of opinions but a certain disposition which reveals itself in contacts with new phenomena and consists in encouraging and welcoming diversity in human life. On the other hand, sympathetic openness modifies our definition of "the fanatic." In this view, the fanatic is transformed. The fanatic is no longer a person with excessive, religious or quasi-religious, and usually mistaken enthusiasm for a certain system of beliefs. Since the sympathetically open person is self-defined as one who approves and works for diversity, then by contrast, the fanatic is someone who acts and speaks against diversity as an organizing principle, someone who does not necessarily hold one set of opinions and launch a crusade to impose it on others but who opposes egalitarian diversity in principle and who chooses some form of hierarchy in social life as a necessity.

Because both tolerance and fanaticism reveal themselves, in real life, as tendencies and dispositions (the first for milder and the second for stricter criteria of selection of acceptable societal ideals), it is argued that all those who cherish the value of diversity must perceive those who even consider subjecting the plurality of ideals to selection and hierarchical organization to be intolerant. According to such reasoning, one does not have to try very hard to be vulnerable to the charge of intolerance to diversity. Thus, the growth of the pluralistic order is likely to increase the number of suspicions of fanaticism. The more diverse the world, the greater the probability that any statement, act, thought, or idea will be regarded as a expression of the intention to exclude, patronize, limit, subject, discriminate.

The pluralistic liberal who is enchanted with diversity, despite repeated declarations that the pluralistic world serves the cause of truth better than any other system, paradoxically has no difficulty in accepting the assumption shared by Marx, Lenin, Foucault, and many others: Truth is primarily a partisan weapon; it is power or a regime rather than a theoretical concept. Therefore dispersing truth is a matter as urgent as dispersing power. In their struggle against the concentration of truth, pluralist liberals argue that analogous to the plurality of the centers of power there are

just as many possible versions of truth. Their argument is undoubtedly in-
genious, and it serves the same purpose as the postmodern assault on the
concept of the center itself. The ultimate aim of those who resort to this argument is not to facilitate the exchange of ideas in order to have a better
and truer understanding of the world but, in their view, to prevent the
emergence of any dominant truth-power structure, to fight fanaticism.

Contemporary toleration has ceased to be what it once was—a practical
skill that enabled people to live together—and has become a complex theoretical issue. Just as negative toleration was in theory and practice insol-
ubly linked with several human virtues and vices, so positive toleration
seems closely connected with several political ideals: justice, diversity,
equality, liberty, fraternity. Yet this latter association is a most dubious
one. It is relatively easy to demonstrate that negative toleration can hu-
manize the political order, but it is a much greater challenge to posit a
complex theory of a superior political system built on the idea of positive
toleration. Since it is agreed that negative toleration has indeed human-
ized the political order, it must also be agreed that it is possible to settle
essential questions and differences about political order and philosophy
irrespective of the question of positive toleration (although toleration may
add to the value of particular solutions). Yet in the face of such evidence,
efforts to connect positive toleration with actual political ideals continue
to imply that the concept of positive toleration itself contains a comprehensive set of fundamental philosophical assertions.

There would be nothing obviously wrong in maintaining a political
philosophy that serves the cause of toleration, were it not that it involves
a deception. If we fail to keep in mind the distinction between negative
and positive toleration, we may easily be misled into believing that both
make the same demands of us. The deception lies in the assertion that a
political philosophy of toleration or, more precisely, *the ideology of toleration*, conveys nothing more than a minimal requirement. Its supporters
want to persuade us that only a minor concession related to an outer form
of behavior—as negative toleration is—is necessary: We should be civilized, compassionate, open, flexible, well-mannered. In fact, the requirements of the ideal of tolerance are maximalist, and the expected concessions are anything but minor. It is no trifle that, as postmodernism
teaches, we are to renounce basic philosophical categories and throw traditional belief in the essential meaningfulness of the world into the dustbin of history. It is no trifle that, as pluralist libertarians insist, we are forbidden to discriminate between different ideals and, in the case of their
conflict, we must distribute them equally.

The deception lies in the way the advocates of positive toleration make
sweeping philosophical statements while at the same time refusing to admit they are making them. Postmodernism, for example, blurs the dis-

tinction, to use Rorty's phrase, between democracy and philosophy. One does not know whether the postmodernists propound a highly controversial philosophical thesis that objective truth does not exist, or whether they are arguing that toleration and pluralism require that there *be* no objective truth. In the first case, the thesis cannot be proven, since the criterion of truth on which such a proof could be built has been destroyed. In the second case, the argument becomes irrelevant because toleration is a form of behavior, not a philosophical hypothesis favoring one model of metaphysics rather than another. Uneasiness about the antimetaphysical revolution is countered with the assertion of the world's pluralistic nature. Any defense of some form of hierarchy in social life is met with the idea of a centerless metaphysics.

The essential trouble with positive toleration (especially in its "sympathetic openness" version) is that it attempts to combine two attitudes which are extremely difficult to reconcile. First, it implies that one can have one's own point of view; second, that one must accept a world of diversity where all points of view are equal (except those that are "fanatical"). Logically, such a combination leads to insoluble conflicts. The possession of a point of view presupposes a certain hierarchy; certain ideas and attitudes have been found right and deserving of sympathy; others found to be tolerable; still others to be wrong, dangerous, and repulsive. The supporters of sympathetic openness imply that one is not entitled to such hierarchies. The absence of effective hierarchies implies that one is forbidden to do two things. First, one is virtually prohibited from making any negative judgments about other points of view because such negative evaluations could be considered discriminatory. (In the case of negative toleration, certain critical evaluations were also discouraged or prevented but for different reasons: out of hypocrisy, humility, good manners, intellectual honesty, and so on.) One is forced to respect something which, contrary to his deepest convictions, he finds distasteful. One is also prohibited from strong self-identification. To be true to the demands of sympathetic openness or postmodern antifoundationalism, one should not identify oneself without simultaneously adding a list of qualifications to dispel any suspicion of harboring an exclusive or closed character. For instant, a truly tolerant Christian would be bound to affirm: "Yes, I am Christian, but I am nevertheless sympathetically open to an artist who puts the Crucifix in urine."

One must ask: Can we live with those two prohibitions? I think the answer is, "No." One cannot be, for example, a Catholic and not feel outrage at a view of the Crucifix in urine. I see, however, one possible way for both prohibitions to be accepted. One would have to develop a certain frame of mind, or even a certain worldview, detached from any traditional hierarchical points of view such as Judaism, Islam, Protestantism, Catholicism, nationalism, conservatism, socialism, and so on. To put it briefly, one would have to become a *Homo liberalis*, whose first and foremost loyalty in public as well as in private is to the order of diversity, not to any one particular creed; someone who strongly believes in the equality of cultures, moralities, ideals, usually because he feels they are authentic expressions of human existence; someone who compensates for the lack of hierarchy (that is, egalitarianism) by resolutely and vehemently opposing all forms of hierarchical outlooks, which are simply defined as "fanaticism"; someone who compensates for the indefiniteness of his creed by espousing different causes at different times (whichever are currently fashionable, his adversaries would not hesitate to remark). One day he will defend AIDS victims; another day he will speak against the oppression of women in Muslim countries; another day he will sign a petition against the anti-abortion law in Ireland.

Homo liberalis constitutes a distinct conception of humanness, and as with every such conception, good and bad things can be said about it. Whether it is preferable to other conceptions of the human person is here beside the point. What is important is that *Homo liberalis* is the only embodiment of humanity that can satisfy the requirements of and conditions for toleration (understood as sympathetic openness), as the particular conception of man advocated by the postmodern version. This is the major and, I would say, irredeemable weakness of sympathetic openness and postmodernism. The principle merit of toleration in the original sense was that a Protestant was not compelled to renounce his Protestantism, and a Jew was not compelled to renounce his Jewishness. It appears now that to earn the honor of being counted among the tolerant we must all become *Homines liberales* and substantially transform our worldviews. Moreover, we must do so not because those worldviews have been proven false but because they are believed to be socially and politically offensive. In short, toleration entails a program of profound social re-education. Of course, such a program may be a good thing in itself or may lead to beneficial results, but why call it toleration? A society which consists of *Homines liberales* may be more tolerant than any of the actually existing societies. This does not mean, however, that it is better than those societies, or that it in the end is worth pursuing at all cost, or that the means which lead to such an end are those of tolerance.

Positive tolerationists ignore the role of strong identities and of strong thought in the functioning of social order. Like Mill, they think that stable identities and stable thought are enemies of freedom. Sometimes—it would be hard to deny—they undoubtedly are. On the other hand, they give us a sense of security and self-assuredness which are necessary ingredients of responsible and predictable social behavior. There is certainly some correlation between self-confidence, deriving from an awareness of the opportunity to rely on norms believed to be stable and valid, and civility, with which one may approach other points of view. Similarly, rootlessness, instability, and identity crises often jeopardize the harmony of political coexistence of groups and individuals. The most dangerous form of nationalism, for example, xenophobic and intolerant (in the original sense), is one that feeds on self-doubt and confusion. For this reason, well-integrated communities, just like well-integrated individuals, are better partners of coexistence than those whose sense of integration has been weakened. Temporary stability founded on such weakness may very well collapse under the pressure of untamed longings, first thwarted and then reborn, for distinct collective identities and for strong philosophies that would give them a relatively durable legitimacy.

Strong identities and strong thought should not be put in radical opposition to toleration for another reason. The category of toleration was conceived precisely for handling the problems that arise out of the clash of strong identities and strong *Weltanschauungen*. Toleration was not a solution to these problems but a way of life where no such solution—on a theoretical as well as on a structural level—seemed at hand. Where strong identities and strong thought are abolished, toleration ceases to be necessary because the original problem it was proposed to cope with no longer exists. If we agree with such enthusiasts of the postmodern weakening as Zygmut Bauman, who claims that in our times "the universal existential mode" is "the experience of estrangement" and that rootlessness and strangeness have become universal to the point of dissolution ("if everyone is a stranger, no one is"), then the question of toleration becomes immaterial. What can intolerance consist of, if we are all not only rootless, homeless, estranged but also satisfied with our new existential condition, having lost the illusions of traditional metaphysics? Where in the new world of thin, provisional, easily changeable and pluralistic identities would it be possible to find a source of discrimination?

Here we are once again confronted with the paradox: In a world constructed so that there should be less and less intolerance, the obsession with its danger increases. The postmodernists and the pluralists, as one might suspect, have not called off their crusade for toleration, nor are they willing to modify its maximalist ambitions. No less than their predecessors, convinced of the imminence of the new era of ultimate toleration, they perceive the danger that supposedly comes from those who do not share their belief in weak identities and weak thought. It would, however, never occur to them that those enemies of the new civilization—"neofascisms" and "new archaisms," as G. B. Madison called them—still exist. Fortunately the real world continues to frustrate, as it has so often in the past, the expectations of enlightened minds. Obviously we do not know what will be, if there is such a thing, the final outcome. Perhaps those enemies—absolutists, foundationalists, essentialists, traditionalists, monists—will lose the battle and be heard from no longer. Perhaps they will become a tiny minority in a world of universal rootlessness and ever increasing diversity and perform the role of eccentrics, which the old liberals thought would be perennially performed by anticonservatives. Perhaps their importance will grow. Perhaps the postmodernists and the pluralists tend to be somewhat hysterical about fanaticism precisely because they have never really believed that their ideal of openness and centerlessness will materialize.

No matter what happens, one thing seems unquestionable. With the continuing struggle for positive toleration in our ways of thinking, of writing, of teaching, of transmitting knowledge, of using certain words and avoiding others; with the continuing emphasis on disenchanted rootlessness and diversity as the metaphysical (or rather antimetaphysical) safeguard of toleration; with the continuing suspicion and fear of partisanship in philosophy and knowledge in general, it may very well be that the world will indeed become more tolerant. At the same time, the things that will be said or allowed to be said about the world will be less and less interesting.

NOTE

"The Trouble with Toleration," by Ryszard Legutko, first appeared in *Partisan Review* LXI, no. 4 (1994): 610–23. Reprinted by permission.

3

✛

Plato's Two Democracies

The description of the degeneration of regimes in the *Republic* is a strikingly perceptive part of the dialogue, yet it provokes little controversy among the commentators. In the major works on the *Republic*, the comments on the degeneration argument occupy relatively little space.[1] In this essay I aim to interpret this Platonic argument and to place it within a larger context of Plato's political philosophy.

Let us start by describing two peculiarities that distinguish Plato's democracy from the types of constitutions that characterized all the previous stages: aristocracy, timocracy, and oligarchy. The first distinction, usually accepted in the commentaries, is that properly speaking democracy is not a constitution at all;[2] the second, rather ignored by the commentators, is that there are in fact two concepts of democracy in this part of the dialogue. In the final sections of this essay, I will give my own interpretation of the role of the nonconstitution in Plato's argument.

Until democracy emerged, the transitions from one regime to another were—to use a modern expression—of an evolutionary or rather devolutionary character:[3] They were slow and without violent political upheavals. The transition from aristocracy to timocracy—which has its ultimate cause in cosmological cycles—as well as the transition from timocracy to oligarchy, were both primarily triggered by a factor of wealth. In the first case it was the party of wealth that in its conflict with the party of honor managed to make a compromise sanctioning private property; and while the lovers of honor had the political power and dominated the life of a community, it was the initial compromise instituting private property that set a stage for an evolutionary process changing people's mores and attitudes. "And thus striving and struggling with one another, they compromise on a middle way: They distribute the land and houses as private property, enslave and hold as serfs and servants those whom they previously guarded as free friends and providers of upkeep" (547b-c, GR).[4] The political power was limited to an external control and superficial forms of behavior; what really mattered—and Plato sounds here almost like a modern socialist—was property or lack thereof. Although, Plato says, the timocratic community likes warfare, its members "will desire money just as those in oligarchies do, passionately adoring gold and silver in secret. They will possess private treasuries and storehouses, where they can keep it hidden, and have houses to enclose them, like private nests, where they can spend lavishly either on women or on anyone else they wish. . . . They'll be mean with their own money, since they value it and are not allowed to acquire it openly, but they'll love to spend other people's because of their appetites" (548a-b, GR).

It is noteworthy that Plato describes the transitions on the example of generations within a family. What in parents' character is hidden or not fully developed, what mitigates their behavior, namely, a legacy of attachment to "goodness and traditional ways" (547b, W), the children consciously reject, identifying themselves with the new ways. The timocratic children break off with the tradition seeing that their fathers, morally good but lacking a competitive spirit, become losers in the eyes of wives, servants, and other citizens. Fearing that they meet with similar contempt the children decide to imitate those forms of behavior that bring success and guarantee social acceptance. In the case of the oligarchic children the process of change is analogous. They see that their fathers' political prestige and honor does not give them real power: They can easily lose the titles, be banished or killed, and have their property confiscated. The sons therefore turn "to tawdry commercial activities, and gradually accumulate wealth by thrift and hard work" (553c, W). They would not let themselves get involved in political struggle for prestige, glory, and honors; they would rather satisfy themselves with a less conspicuous and less risky aspect of success: personal wealth.

The process of devolution that starts with aristocracy has a clear logic. In the course of the changes, the principle of government—which at the beginning was a unity—undergoes disintegration. Gradually, various factors that constituted it begin to disappear as a result of the destructive impact of wealth and of all those desires with which it is correlated. First, wisdom and intellectual qualities decline, then honor and military virtues, and finally an interest in art, culture, and education.

When democracy comes in, the principle of government practically ceases to exist. The final stages of oligarchy lead to the virtual destruction of the political sphere, and ultimately, with all unifying bonds expunged, of the state itself. What emerges is precisely the phenomenon of which Plato warned at the outset of his political argument in the *Republic*: When there is no sense of the community, particular groups, usually differentiated according to wealth, will regard themselves as different "states," that is, they will be totally separated from each other, treating each other as enemies (422e–423b). The two "states" thus form themselves—the rich and the poor. As the former lose the political will to govern and degenerate into creatures "too soft and lazy to resist pleasure and pain" (556c, W), the poor, seeing their enemies' "breathlessness and utter ineptitude" (556d, W), make a revolution—either killing their enemies or forcing them into exile (557a)—and seize power.[5]

But the revolutionary character of this act does not reveal itself only in the abruptness of the political change and the deep cleavage between the two hostile parties. With the democratic revolution, the nature of the system undergoes a radical transformation. Whereas the previous societies were constitutions, albeit imperfect ones, democracy is, in real terms, a nonconstitution; it becomes anarchy, i.e., a society with no government, no authority, no law, no principle that could organize political life. It is no longer a community in a meaningful sense of the world, as social bonds—particularly those that constitute a family—also cease to exist.

In this, democracy may be compared to the next and final stage of the degeneration—tyranny. The latter also establishes itself through a political takeover, rather than through a gradual change in the mentality of a new generation. The masses "set up one man as their special champion" (565c) who demands "a bodyguard to keep their defender safe for them" (566b). Having been granted this, he brings down "many others [and] . . . stands in the city's chariot, a complete tyrant rather than a leader" (566d, GR).

Tyranny, like democracy, also marks a qualitative change in the process of degeneration. Whereas democracy signified a shift from constitution to anarchy, that is, from the political to the nonpolitical, tyranny is a regime that pushes the degeneration even further down: from the human to the nonhuman. Plato describes a tyrant as someone who is "transformed from a man into a wolf" (566a), having a "beastly and savage" mind (571c, GR), tasting "human innards" (565d) and "kindred blood" (565e), having "dangerous, wild and lawless" desires (572b, GR). If the tyrant can be compared to a human being, then he will be a beastlike creature, "a drunk lustful maniac," a person "insane and mentally disturbed try[ing] to dominate the gods, let alone other human beings, and expect[ing] to be able to do so" (573c), someone who "in his dreams . . . doesn't stop at trying to have sex with his mother and with anyone or anything else—man, beast, or god," someone who is "ready to slaughter anything" and who "doesn't hold back from anything, however bizarre or disgusting" (571c–d, W).

The whole process of degeneration has thus three distinct stages. The first, which covers aristocracy, timocracy, and oligarchy, consists of a gradual disintegration of the original system. The second, starting with the last phase of oligarchy and culminating in democracy, is a state of anarchy where no common and stable political principles are accepted. The third, tyranny, is a state where power reappears but in a perverse form, and where not only the political but also the moral principles on which human nature is based are rejected.

The second peculiarity about the notion of democracy in the *Republic* is that it is not consistent with everything Plato said about this regime. The one sketched above, anarchy, has its alternative in a somewhat different system, which is a populist democracy, politically and economically stratified, and certainly not devoid of government. Plato speaks about it at length in the section describing the last phase of democracy leading do tyranny. The democratic society has three classes: the "drones," politically active, who effectively hold the government in their hands; the wealthy who are "the most disciplined" and who therefore succeed financially (564e); and finally, "the general populace—the smallholders, who do not spend all their time on politics and do not have a great deal of property," who form "the largest section of the population, and when they gather in one spot they are the most authoritative group in a democracy" (565a, W). In a certain respect this regime resembles an oligarchy: There are two major economic classes—the rich and the poor (the idlers do not count economically). The difference is that the poor have the ultimate power. They do not make a frequent use of it, but when they do, it has an enormous impact: It is they who bring democracy into being by overthrowing oligarchy, and it is they who contribute to its destruction when, afraid of the oligarchic restoration, they appoint a leader and give him power to crush, in the defense of their interests, a real or imagined plot of a rich minority. Just as the poor tolerate the rich, possibly having confidence in their own ultimate superiority, they also tolerate the fact that the actual management of the affairs is in the hands of the "drones." The last group does not satisfy itself with action; it is also a party of "speaking," which means that it articulates the opinions that might affect political life. There is thus a clear division of spheres: The majority have the ultimate political power, the minority has economic wealth, the idlers make the particular decisions and also have what one might call ideological power, that is, they produce and control opinions.

This type of democracy differs in at least two important respects from anarchy. First, it has a clear structure and—to a certain point—a fairly stable form of government. The relation between the rich and the poor is certainly not that between two hostile "states" or societies, as was the case in the last stage of oligarchy. Nothing Plato says would suggest such hostility, and some things he says exclude it: The poor are not interested in politics, being rightly convinced that they hold the ultimate power, while the rich are "disciplined" and seem to have no political ambitions. The only group that is potentially outside the system are the drones. Plato uses this name to denote the people who do not have any positive links with, nor make any positive contribution to, the political community, even a contribution as modest in Plato's eyes as the creation of wealth. From the point of view of the state they are useless and even, as an alien and destructive element, dangerous. One has the impression that were it not for the drones and for the poor's tolerant attitude towards them (Plato suggests people "should try to eradicate them as quickly as possible, cells and all" [564c, W]), the regime might have a longer life. Still, in spite of the menacing presence of the drones, populist democracy has a certain limited degree of viability that stems from the peacefulness of the two main social groups as well as from the unquestionable authority of one of them.

What has been said about this type of democracy does not apply to anarchy. Anarchical democracy does not have a tripartite, let alone dual structure, but is a society of thriving pluralism where no particular group or person holds power or even occupies a dominant position. No group interest is likely to emerge in a society characterized by "colorful variety," like "a cloak . . . adorned with every species of flower" (557c, W). In fact this society is ruled by egalitarian sentiments so deep that it eventually abolishes the hierarchical distinctions between free men and slaves, parents and children, teachers and students, men and women, people and animals. There is no indication in Plato's text that these developments occur only among the drones; it is clear that the democratic man represents the character, opinions, and attitudes that, if not typical, are at least considered attractive by the majority of the population.

Second, in populist democracy ruled by the poor the economic factor plays an essential role, both as a source of identification and as an ideological ploy to mobilize one group of the society against the other. With politics left in the hands of the drones, the rest of the population is busy trying to acquire wealth. "Everyone is trying to make money," writes Plato (564e), in the context of the few rich, who do best financially because of their discipline. The majority are less successful but the economic motive is so important for them that, unwilling as they are to make use of their ultimate authority, they decide to do so whenever "there's honey to be gained" (565a). This allows the "drones," i.e., the democratic leaders, to enrich themselves: They "rob the rich and distribute the trivial amounts they don't keep for themselves to the general populace" (565a). The essential role of the economic factor does not square with the anarchistic form of democracy. The democratic man living in a society of "colorful variety" is a person of many desires and aspirations, wealth being one of them, and certainly not a privileged one. He insists, Plato writes, that desires "are all alike and of equal value," and his life is a perfect illustration of this. "He indulges in every passing desire that each day brings. One day he gets drunk at a party, the next day he's sipping water and trying to lose weight; then again, he sometimes takes exercise, sometimes takes things easy without a care in the world, and sometimes he is apparently a student of philosophy. At frequent intervals, he gets involved in community affairs, and his public speaking and other duties keep him leaping around here, there, and everywhere. If military types arouse his admiration, he inclines towards the military life; if it is businessmen, he is all for business. His lifestyle had no rhyme or reason, but he thinks it enjoyable, free, and enviable and he never dispenses with it" (561c–d, W).

Plato—let me make it clear—did not make those two regimes utterly separated. In the beginning and in the end phases of democracy they seem to converge. When the poor made the revolution, they acted both self-assertively, securing their economic and political interests, and also carried the banner of general emancipation. "So democracy starts when the poor are victorious. They kill some of the rich. They expel others, and they give everyone who's left equal social and political rights" (557a, W). The poor, living in deprivation and misery, seem to be motivated by some kind of universalistic egalitarian-libertarian ideology that they attempt to put into practice after they have seized power. Similarly, at the end the mechanisms of both regimes converge. The excessive liberty typical of anarchy makes the drones a powerful group, which in turn enables them to subvert the shaky balance between the rich and the poor in populist democracy, which leads to tyranny. Where the two regimes clearly diverge is the middle phase: Between the rampant pluralism of anarchy and the tripartite system of populist democracy there seems to be no common ground. Even if we interpret those two democracies as phases of a single process, this will still leave unchallenged the thesis about their structural differences.

Of these two regimes the former seems more puzzling. The latter, populist democracy, is a well-known concept in Greek political thought. Although Plato may have given it an original interpretation, the basic elements are not new. The economic division of the society (even if for the Greeks the terms "the poor" and "the rich" had also a noneconomic meaning, i.e., educated and non-educated), group interest prevailing over the interest of the state, ultimate power's lying with the majority (as contrasted with the regimes ruled by a minority and by one man), the poor's being manipulated by the demagogues, all these ideas recur in most of the depictions of democracy in ancient writers from Pseudo-Xenophon to Aristotle.

Anarchistic democracy is a far more original notion. By distinguishing it from populist democracy, Plato may have stumbled here upon the modern distinction between liberal and democratic orders. This is all the more surprising because, as some commentators argue, a liberal approach to politics does not represent Athenian experience. "If parts of his description are aimed at contemporary Athens," writes Julia Annas with unconcealed irritation, "they miss. Plato presents democracy as defined by tolerant pluralism, but Athens was a populist democracy, with a clearly defined way of life separating those with power from those without, and about as tolerant of openly expressed nonconformity as McCarthyite America."[6] Despite a somewhat misplaced comparison, Annas's remark poses an important question: What type of experience was behind this rather unusual, by contemporary Greek standards, description of democracy?

No less amazing is the fact that Plato's attitude to this regime is far from unequivocal. He may be mocking the extreme forms of equality, writing about the dogs that start to resemble their mistresses, and about horses and donkeys that learn "to strut about with absolute freedom, bumping into anyone they meet on the road who doesn't get out of the way" (563c, W). He might find grotesque the decline of authority in family and in school where "the older members of the community adapt themselves to the younger ones, ooze frivolity and charm, and model their behavior on that of the young, because they don't want to be thought disagreeable tyrants" (563a–b, W). All this, however, does not change the overall impression that Plato is not as critical of democracy as he should be considering its clearly low position on the scale of degeneration. Definitely he is not as critical of democracy as he has been, say, of oligarchy—theoretically, a less corrupted regime. Crombie maintains that "Plato's sentiments did not obey his reason, and it is evident that he despises the oligarchic man, whereas, about the democratic man, he says that such a man sometimes manages to find a place for all his desires, and becomes a man of great versatility. Of one who thus succeeds Plato says that he becomes "agreeable, free, and blessed"; I do not find it easy to take this simply as sarcasm. Socrates, after all, had "loved Alcibiades."[7] Whether Plato is really divided between his emotional and philosophical judgments remains to be seen, but Crombie is undoubtedly right that sarcasm cannot exhaust the philosopher's attitude to democracy. The versatility that characterizes the democratic man, even if superficial and sometimes caricatural, is not to be easily dismissed. Contrary to other human types the man in democracy has all parts of his soul active. One may deplore that they are not made proper use of, but one cannot doubt that they are at least partly capable of influencing people's behavior. In particular, the democratic man still has some interest in philosophy and is not insensitive to higher aspirations.

Also worth reflecting upon is the fact that unlike populist democracy, the anarchy seems to have no obvious logical place within the structure of the degeneration passage and of the whole argument of the *Republic*. That populist democracy has such a place is fairly obvious. Viewed in a broader perspective this regime is simply a continuation of the struggle for wealth that since the first cleavage in the aristocratic system had been the essential motive in the process of degeneration. The revolution that established this system was to achieve what the previous systems were incapable of achieving, namely, to give access to wealth to the majority of the population. It not only failed in that respect but created such a potential for further wealth-based conflicts that it finally resulted in the destruction of the human relations among the members of the society.

Viewed from an even larger perspective—that of the whole dialogue—populist democracy also has a clear function. The aim of the dialogue was, remember, to grasp such a system of justice that would be true in itself, and unlike all political and moral systems existing so far, would not depend on the interest or benefit of the dominating party. From the moment of Glaucon's and Adeimantus' interventions in Book II it became clear that Plato had formulated his concept of justice against the whole Greek tradition that, he thinks, glorifies the domination and power and that, therefore, contains a poisonous seed of tyranny. Populist democracy was thus another version of a system built on domination, where the disease was so widespread that the only possible development at this stage could be tyranny in its pure form.

Pluralistic democracy does not seem to fit into those perspectives as it promotes neither a struggle for wealth nor a struggle for power. What, then, is its place in the argument? Does the regime cultivating colorful variety have any role to play in the argument, or should we rather see in it, as Crombie suggested, a proof that Plato, despite his critical animus, was unable to sever his emotional links with the democratic tradition; or perhaps, as Annas implied, the rampant pluralism is a caricature of those few elements of freedom that miraculously survived in the essentially intolerant Athenian democracy? I do not think there is an obvious and definite solution of this problem. I will however try to argue for an answer that I think has some plausibility; namely, that pluralistic democracy, as conceived by Plato, is not only a stage in degeneration but also satisfies the essential condition required for the process of political regeneration. In other words, I will argue that if Plato ever thought of reversing the corruption of the regimes and intended, ultimately, to build the philosopher's state, he could conceive of pluralistic democracy as a society in which such a process might start.

One of the basic conditions that, according to Plato, must be fulfilled for the political reform to succeed is a social and political tabula rasa. He mentions this notion twice in the *Republic*: The ruling philosophers

> must treat a community and people's characters like a painting-board, and their first job is to wipe it clean. This isn't a particularly easy thing to do, but you'll appreciate that the main way they differ from everyone else is in refusing to deal with an individual or a community, and not being prepared to sketch out a legal code, until they've either been given a clean slate or have made it so themselves. . . . I imagine the next stage would involve their constantly looking this way and that as they work—looking on the one hand towards that which is inherently moral, right, self-disciplined, and so on, and on the other hand towards what they're creating in the human realm. (501a–b, W)
>
> First, they [the ruling philosophers] banish everyone over the age of ten into the countryside. Then they take charge of the community's children and make sure that they're beyond the reach of existing conventions, which their parents adhere to, are similar to the ones we were describing before. (540e–541a, W)

Of all regimes characterized in the *Republic* pluralist democracy comes closest to the "clean slate" condition. Whereas other regimes reflected, in increasingly diluted form, the original idea of the best regime, in pluralist democracy there is no trace of the original order left. It is, politically speaking, an institutional vacuum, a zero state, from which we can either go further down—and this would be falling below the human level, as illustrated by tyranny—or, theoretically at least, go up, trying to rebuild the institutions in the right way.

The "clean slate" in democracy may be understood both negatively and positively. Negatively it would mean that the democratic society is amorphous and thus ready to take any form that is imposed on it. Having no institution and no political life in the proper sense, it allows the reformer to take the steps that other regimes would not allow. In other words, democracy is like building material that in the hands of the ruler will transform itself, without resistance from the democratic men, into an architectural construction. Plato may have implied here that democratic disintegration, though essentially a deplorable process, has at least one positive consequence that puts democracy above other less imperfect regimes. Those regimes may be more ordered, but they are also inherently one-sided, whereas the disintegrated chaos has laid bare all elements that were constitutive of the initial order. Under pluralist democracy all political tendencies are present, all desires and aspirations of human soul are potentially available, and—one may hope—all, under propitious conditions, may be made beneficial use of.

This notion of pluralist democracy as building material for a better regime has another side to it. Let us note that Plato never mentions coercion as a necessary measure, as if excluding the possibility that the ruler will have to resort to drastic means. In this the *Republic* differs from Plato's later political dialogues, for instance from the *Statesman,* where such drastic means seem to belong to a natural procedure of the ruler (293c–d, 308e–309a). This exclusion of the coercive measures makes sense only with respect to pluralist democracy. If Plato says that the philosopher-king should "take charge of the community's children and make sure that they're beyond the reach of existing conventions, which their parents adhere to," this, when applied to oligarchy or timocracy, would mean a drastic assault on the institution of family. In pluralist democracy such a step does not seem particularly brutal as the institution of family—at least as Plato sees it—has practically ceased to exist. The same is true of the other social hierarchies, which retained some viability from the original system and which under democracy disintegrated into omnipresent egalitarian amorphousness.

Looked at differently, the pluralist society may resemble a child or a young man who is still amorphous in the sense of being as yet unformed and uneducated, but who has many possibilities that may be actualized—not through coercion, but through education. Indeed Plato himself calls democracy "a beautiful and youthful regime" (563e3–4).[8] This naïve lightheartedness of the democratic life that Plato often portrays with irony could of course have a sinister aspect. While it is true that from this "beautiful and youthful regime tyranny grows," it may be no less true that democratic youthfulness, like any other form of youthfulness, gives some prospect of hope. It is probably this aspect of democracy—absent in other more mature, and therefore more rigid and less malleable regimes—that mitigated Plato's harsh critique of pluralism.

The "clean slate" of pluralist democracy may also have a more positive meaning: not only a state of amorphousness but a certain inclination. The pluralist society is, Plato says, full of *exousia* where everyone "will arrange his own life in whatever manner pleases him" (557b, GR). The word *exousia*, meaning either *licentia* or *potestas*, suggests that this regime not only lifts the prohibitions or obstacles that stand in the way of human endeavors, but also provides people with opportunities to materialize their plans. This is said by Socrates in the context of the democratic men who do not have coherent and far-reaching plans. Whether this would also apply to a situation when the philosopher-king tries to reorganize the system totally is of course uncertain, but Plato's words do not exclude such a possibility.

The *exousia* in democratic pluralism, he says, makes possible political experiments. This system is, properly speaking, not one political regime, but many regimes being in the state of constant experimentation: It is, Plato says, a sort of general store for political systems (557d), i.e., a society in which various forms of human cooperation are being tried, and none, even the democratic, becomes the prevailing one. This should also give a chance, however slim, to philosophy-inspired serious reformers. Democracy is, in Socrates' words that seem to support this hope, "a convenient place to look for a constitution . . . because it contains all kinds of constitutions on account of the license it gives its citizens. So it looks as though anyone who wants to put a city in order, as we were doing, should probably go to a democracy, as to a supermarket of constitutions, pick out whatever pleases him, and establish that" (557b, GR). This need not mean that if the philosopher tried to establish his regime in a democracy, he would naturally find acceptance and obedience among the citizens. It may mean however that at least among some members of the pluralist society, if anywhere at all, a philosopher may find a sympathetic ear, because it is in this society, not in any other, that we encounter some understanding for philosophy.[9] And since the understanding for philosophy and for the authority of reason are the essential prerequisites of political regeneration, the democratic man is the most promising, if not the only possible, addressee of the philosopher-king's message.

But how effective, one might ask, will be the philosophical influence on people engaged in democratic politics? Those who argue (from Aristotle onwards) that Plato misinterpreted the nature of political order that, contrary to what he says, is based on practical rather than philosophical knowledge, on habits rather than on reflection, are of course right, except that the society about which he spoke and against which he directed his critique was of a somewhat different kind. This was the society exposed to the power of *logoi*, the society where the general concepts were in constant use. From the early dialogues on Plato was portraying the democratic men who acted under the spell of those concepts and whose political behavior usually was *logos*-oriented. True, the meanings given to those concepts, as Socrates was never tired of pointing out, were inconsistent, instrumental, arbitrary; what is remarkable however is that the *logoi*—in the large sense of the term—seemed to have more power in politics than inherited social practices, habits, or tacit conventions. This may help us to answer the question that emerged from the doubts that Annas had about Plato's parody of the tolerant society: What social experience was behind pluralist democracy in the *Republic*? Even if the democratic Athens did not have the "colorful variety" of this regime and was much less tolerant, it had a large degree of intellectual diversity that was the result of the incessant use of *logoi*. In no other system was there such abundance of argumentativeness and such a widespread commitment to political and social self-assertion through *logos*.

Obviously from this plurality of arguments, chaotic and probably philosophically useless from the Platonic point of view, there is a closer distance to the world of the sophists than to the philosopher-king's state. A lot has been written, by Plato himself and by his commentators, about the hostility between the philosopher and a democratic mob: the former unwilling "to go down again to the prisoners in the cave and share their labors and honors, whether they are of less worth or of greater" (519d4–7), the latter unwilling to go up and ready to kill "anyone who tried to free them and lead them upward" (517a5–6, GR). At the same time however, there are a few passages where Plato seems less dramatic, and somewhat backs down on the notion of the irreconcilability of philosophy and politics. He observes, for example, that philosophy "despite her present poor state . . . is still more prestigious than other occupations"; when it is left "vacated," "desolate and unwed," it falls prey to "little men . . . who leap gladly from those little crafts to philosophy, like prisoners escaping from jail who take refuge in a temple" (495c–d, GR). When philosophy falls into disrepute in the society or is considered useless, it is often because the wrong people take possession of her while the right ones fall away from her.

As for the majority of citizens, they are not entirely insensitive to the philosophical arguments and should not be ignored as potential recipients of intellectual wisdom. When Adeimantus imputes to them a less than enthusiastic attitude to the philosopher's state, Socrates admonishes him: "You should not make such wholesale charges against the majority, for they'll no doubt come to a different opinion, if instead of indulging your love of victory at their expense, you soothe them and try to remove their slanderous prejudice against the love of learning, by pointing out what you mean by a philosopher and by defining the philosophic nature and way of life, as we did just now, so that they'll realize that you don't mean the same people as they do" (499e–500a, GR). It is symptomatic that this statement appears immediately after Plato's reflection on the feasibility of the philosopher's regime, which he concludes with a remark: "[I]t is not impossible for this to happen and we are not speaking of impossibilities. That it is difficult for it to happen, however, we agree ourselves" (499d4–6, GR).

A question arises how Plato could reconcile this picture of the democratic society with the one he usually draws: that of a thoughtless mob. A possible explanation may be that, envisaging two concepts of democracy, he also envisaged two different images of the majority. One that is blind to philosophy and would rather kill the philosopher than obey him is closer to the majority living under populist democracy, which consists of unsuccessful, wealth-oriented, and envy-ridden individuals. Perhaps Plato had this type of a society in mind when he compared it to "a huge, strong beast" that has changing moods and appetites (493a–b). The other type of the majority, of which he has a more favorable view, is the one that has not entirely lost its respect for philosophy and still considers it to be "a prestigious occupation." Such a majority lives under pluralist democracy and such a majority will be one that, in a situation unlikely but not impossible to come about, will follow the philosopher-king's instructions, and that in another passage Plato calls *polis peithomene*, "a polis that can be persuaded to comply" (502b4-5). And although it would be groundless to make a simple identification of pluralist democracy and *polis peithomene*, it certainly is remarkable that both societies share an important common characteristic: In both, persuasion and arguments may be effective.

If the above analysis is justified, Plato's attitude to democracy is not only a historical phenomenon. Nor is it merely a matter of a textual exegesis that would settle a long-discussed question of the practicability of the philosopher-king's state. There are reasons to believe that what Plato said set a standard for several important arguments that were to animate the debate about the nature and viability of a pluralist order, the debate that reappeared in the postmedieval world and has been going on until today. It would be interesting to trace the reception of Plato's arguments in later political philosophy, but this, of course, is a most complex task, far exceeding the size and framework of this essay. In the concluding paragraphs I will mention only two of those ideas that, I think, were crucial in his critique of pluralist democracy and that did not disappear with the fall of democratic Athens.

Plato was probably the first philosopher to question to what extent the order built on individual liberty and equality as the basic political ideals—let us call it liberal—is negative; that is, to what extent it emerges through the disintegration of traditional, organic social bonds, institutions, and moral practices. Paradoxically, the thinkers who believed that there is a high degree of negativity in this order came from both sides of the debate: the antiliberals like Hegel and Marx, as well as the liberals like Popper. The paradox, however, is only apparent: The antiliberals objected to what the liberals supported. The former criticized the system for having annihilated traditional hierarchies and for having reduced the social fabric to a rational exchange of goods and services; the latter praised the new order for having liberated people from the bondage of the inherited dependencies and for having turned them into free-floating individuals capable of constructing, through their own free decisions, the political and social environment in accordance with their needs. The word *liberation*, let us note, thus meant a process of reducing, as much as possible, all human relations to natural, simple, formal, minimal rules of behavior, with all other rules being rejected, or depreciated, or removed from the public sphere because they express artificial and thus arbitrary structures of power.

This presupposition that a liberal society comes into being as a result of the annihilation of the traditional order rather than as a result of social construction and social evolution poses another question: To what degree do we have, in such a society, *licentia* and *potestas* to have our projects materialized? In other words, to what degree does a liberated society offer no resistance—in the form of inherited social, moral, and political barriers—to our projects and give us sufficient room for implementing the ideals that we choose; to what extent we are free, in the absence of any structural obstacles, to give political life the form we desire? And here again, the answers to this question tend to converge; both liberals and antiliberals seem to have believed that our possibilities of action in a liberated society are incomparably higher than in any other society. On the antiliberal side, Karl Marx went probably as far as one could go. He claimed that the liberal order is a preparatory stage that, after purging the society of feudal anachronisms, will open the way for a fully mature system of communism that will be the culmination of history; we would not, he reiterated, have the blessings of communism and the final consummation of history without the necessary mopping up operation that the liberal bourgeoisie performed on the traditional communities. The argument of the liberal side was different but it, too, appealed to inexhaustible possibilities of the society that broke links with tradition. We already have it in John Stuart Mill, but the most ambitious version is to be found in the works of modern libertarians. A system of liberty is seen as infinitely spacious, not only providing possibilities for all human aspirations but giving each of them a safe niche to develop. In a way this system may also be viewed as the culmination of history and as the ultimate all-encompassing utopia; the difference is that for people like Karl Marx the communist utopia favored only one set of ideas and disqualified all the others, whereas in the libertarian paradise all ideas and projects will find their own safe places.[10]

The second view that was to recur in later political philosophy was, to use Tocqueville's well-known formula, the important role of general concepts in liberal democracy. Plato was obviously not the first who discovered this propensity of the democratic man. Socrates and the sophists had been aware of it, too: Socrates by attempting to give those concepts clear and absolute meanings, the sophists by trying to blur those meanings relating them to social context. What Plato may be claimed to have discovered, however, is the connection, discernible in his description of the pluralist system, between a process of social disintegration and a growing role for general concepts: With the growth of equality and the decline of stable social and moral hierarchies, general concepts tend to take over the function of organizing political life and justifying political divisions. Democratic freedom, Plato explained, created conditions in which philosophy could develop and, one hopes, give a sense of direction to political decisions; unfortunately, philosophy did not perform this function, since it itself became entangled in democratic politics and thus lost its reputation as an independent intellectual activity. Translated into a modern idiom the argument would be: Liberal democracy, though dependent on the abstract categories that, in the absence of traditional practices, express people's aspirations and help them communicate, has an inherent tendency to corrupt them by making them an element of a democratic pursuit of power; therefore those concepts—the ideas of justice, virtue, piety, goodness, beauty—have to be, so to speak, supplied from outside the mechanisms of democracy. They should, Plato thought, be supplied by philosophy viewed as a disinterested pursuit of truth. In other words, Plato posed the question to which the answer is still pending: To what degree can the liberal order be its own judge, and to what degree should it, let alone for the sake of its own survival, submit to some higher, nonliberal and nondemocratic standards?

NOTES

1. Some of the major works that deal with the *Republic* almost entirely ignore this passage: N. R. Murphy, *The Interpretation of Plato's Republic* (Oxford: Clarendon Press, 1960); C.D.C. Reeve, *The Argument of Plato's Republic* (Princeton: Princeton University Press, 1988). Among those that have some comments on it are: Julia Annas, *An Introduction to Plato's Republic* (Oxford: Clarendon Press, 1981), 294–305; Allan Bloom, *The Republic of Plato*, 2nd ed. (New York: Basic Books, 1991), 414–25; Leo Strauss, *The City and Man* (Chicago: University of Chicago Press, 1978), 129–33.

2. "Politically . . . *democracy* stands not for a kind of constitutional government, but for a non-constitutional condition, the only principle of which is to treat all men as equal and to have no other principles." I. M. Crombie, *An Examination of Plato's Doctrines*, vol. I (London: Routledge and Kegan, 1962), 135.

3. Although evolution implies a change for the better rather than for the worse, some translators, notably Waterfield, used, in this context, the verb "to evolve" to render Greek *gignesthai*; see Plato, *Republic*, trans. Robin Waterfield (Oxford: Oxford University Press, 1994).

4. For quotations I alternately use two translations: G.M.A. Grube's revised by C.D.C. Reeve (Indianapolis: Hackett, 1992), and Robin Waterfield's, referred to in the text, respectively, as GR and W.

5. The concept of "revolution" seems to fit in some contexts. Among the translators Shorey makes a frequent use of it; see Plato, *Republic*, trans. Paul Shorey, 2 vols. (Cambridge, Mass.: Harvard University Press, 1935). He uses the expression

"the revolution in the city" to render the phrase *he polis meteballe* (559e4) that describes the democratic seizure of power. He also speaks of oligarchs who under democracy "may have revolutionary designs"—*epithumōsi neoterizein* (565b5–6).

6. Annas, *Introduction to Plato's Republic*, 300. Strauss makes a somewhat similar point when he speaks of "Socrates' exaggeration of the licentious mildness of classical democracy." According to him, "Plato writes as if the Athenian democracy had not carried out Socrates' execution, and Socrates speaks as if the Athenian democracy had not engaged in an orgy of bloody persecution of guilty and innocent alike when the Hermes statues were mutilated at the beginning of the Sicilian expedition" (*The City and Man*, 132).

7. Crombie, *Examination of Plato's Doctrines*, 135.

8. The word *neanikē* means "youthful," but also "vigorous." Most translators prefer the latter meaning, but I do not think there are sufficient grounds for it. While it is easy to argue that democracy is "youthful," I do not see an obvious reason why it should be "vigorous."

9. Bloom aptly observed that "democracy is . . . the only one of the practical regimes in which philosophy makes an appearance. . . . The moral or fiscal austerity of timocracy and oligarchy preclude the leisure necessary to philosophy and condemn the thought produced by it; at the same time, life in these regimes is too organized for philosophy to be able to escape unnoticed for long" (*Republic of Plato*, 421).

10. On this notion of libertarianism see my essay "Society as a Department Store," chapter 1, in this book.

4

✛

On Postmodern
Liberal Conservatism

John Gray is an intriguing writer. His last two collections of essays, *Liberalisms* (New York: Routledge, 1989) and *Post-Liberalism* (New York: Routledge, 1993), contain ample material to justify this opinion. The books explore a rich variety of subjects using several approaches: conceptual analysis, history of ideas, reinterpretation of classic and modern authors, diagnosis of modern political culture, criticisms of the Anglo-American philosophical establishment, and polemics against Marxism. I am afraid I cannot do justice to the many merits of these works and to the brilliance of Gray's arguments on specific issues. So I will ignore all those matters in which I agree with Gray, simply because there are too many of them and because I could not hope to improve on his treatment of them. Instead I will concentrate on the few selected questions, fairly important for Gray as a thinker, where he and I differ. They revolve around his notion of postmodern liberal conservatism and touch upon four points: his belief that we are witnessing the end of both liberalism and all universalist philosophy—in short, the demise of the tradition of thought that began with Socrates and Plato—his theory of objective value pluralism, his conception of civil society, and his interpretation of modern liberal society.

THE END OF PHILOSOPHY?

Much of what Gray objects to in liberalism—and the critique of liberalism is a leitmotif of the two books—is, in my opinion, indeed objectionable. There has been in liberalism a strange mixture of universalist hubris

and philosophical aridity. On the one hand, liberalism has too often suc-
cumbed to a thoughtless disdain for all nonliberal thought and practice,
as if all of history amounts to merely a too slow and never finished
process of emancipation, and as if all philosophical wisdom could be
contained in the latest best-selling liberal publication expressing the most
advanced phase of liberation. On the other hand, there has been an irritating emptiness to liberalism, a tendency to bracket or to reduce to private preferences the answers to basic human dilemmas, while putting in
their place abstractions very remote from what real people actually live
and die for.

Yet although I agree with Gray's general diagnosis of the blind alley in
which modern liberalism finds itself, as well as with many specific details
of his critique of liberalism, I do not share either Gray's premises or his
conclusions. I, too, would like to see liberalism enriched, but I doubt if
this could—or should, for that matter—be achieved in Gray's way.

One thing Gray finds unwarranted and untenable in liberalism is its
universalist ambition. This is a major point in his argument, but it is far
from clear exactly what it means. His thesis, as expounded in *Liberalisms*,
has at least three meanings that lead us in three different directions.

Thesis 1: Liberal universalism is unfounded because "there is within the
diversity of forms of government and society disclosed to us in history a
legitimate variety of frameworks for human well-being." The liberal, who
prides himself on being tolerant, in fact lacks tolerance since his "univer-
salizing doctrinal zeal" leads him to a silly self-centeredness: "all nonliberal societies stand condemned, together with the excellences and
virtues which they harboured" (1989, 239).

Thesis 2: Liberal universalism is unfounded because there are several
liberalisms, not necessarily compatible with one another. "The liberalism of Locke has little in common with that of Mill and it is an error to
see two liberalisms as moments in a continuous historical process." The
result of recent works on the subject has been to effect "a historical deconstruction of liberalism as an intellectual tradition and to retrieve for
us the discontinuities, accidents, variety, and historical concreteness of
the thinkers indifferently lumped together under the label of liberalism"
(1989, 262).

Thesis 3: Liberal universalism is unfounded because one of the lessons
of contemporary experience is a discovery of "the foundationlessness of
the modern project," which, rooted in the Western intellectual tradition,
originated in antiquity. "Not only the project of the Enlightenment, but
also that of the Socratic founders of the very subject are seen to be misconceived. The ruination of the project of a liberal ideology will then be
seen as encompassing the end of an intellectual tradition central to our
self-understanding in the west" (1989, 241).

These are clearly three different sorts of arguments. It is one thing to say liberalism cannot claim universality because it ignores nonliberal contributions to our civilization, and another thing to say that the doctrine itself is inherently particularistic, heterogenous, incohesive, and intrinsically divergent; it is still another thing to say that liberalism cannot be universalized because the whole tradition that made possible a claim to universalism has collapsed.

Moreover, some of the obvious senses in which these three arguments can be understood are unconvincing, if not entirely false: All philosophical theories are to some extent too self-centered, and all suffer from internal fragmentation and inconsistency. As for the end of philosophy, it has been so often announced that it has become a part of philosophical folklore.

I will ignore theses 1 and 2: The first I find accurate and cannot improve upon; the second is, in my opinion, rather uninteresting, for, if accepted, not much follows from it, certainly much less than Gray implies. I think it is worthwhile to devote some space to the third thesis, which I consider presumptuous, because it accounts for a substantial part of both Gray's destructive and constructive projects.

There are important reasons why statements about the end of foundationalist and essentialist classical philosophy should be treated with utmost skepticism. All such claims presuppose some kind of fatalism, with the implication that whoever is foolish enough to adhere today to foundationalist metaphysics will sooner or later find himself in the dustbin of history. In that sense the postmodernists, speaking in the name of irreversible changes, resemble Marxists and, like them, demonstrate a remarkable but ultimately arrogant ease in drawing the line between the old and the new. The development of philosophical thought has shown that there cannot be a final verdict on any type of reflection and on the culture it animates; that revivals, renaissances, and rebirths happen as often as declines and demises; and that since there has not been a definitive collapse of any major orientation for two and a half millennia, it is hard to believe that a collapse is now in progress.

Gray rightly criticizes liberalism for its insensitivity to the value of nonliberal contributions, yet he himself seems to commit a similar mistake. When Gray advises us to respond to a recent philosophical revolution by cutting ourselves off from a large body of philosophical reflection, including ancient Greek and medieval Christian thought, he seems to me to counsel a self-inflicted spiritual and cultural mutilation. It is one thing to be critical of certain trends in the Western intellectual tradition and to look for one's roots outside the philosophical mainstream, and quite another to speak of "the end of an intellectual tradition central to our self-understanding in the west."

Fortunately, Gray as an author, his revolutionary declaration notwithstanding, does not appear to have altogether rejected the legacy of "the Socratic founders"; rather, he seems to be greatly indebted to them. So it is somewhat puzzling that Gray, who does not spare harsh words when speaking about the gurus of American academia responsible for the intellectual fashions that have damaged so much of today's culture and impoverished our philosophical sensibility, seems to be so strongly attracted to one of their favorite ideas. Multiculturalism, for example, a phenomenon of which he emphatically disapproves, is after all a direct descendant of a belief that he shares with "the liberal nomenklatura" and the "culturally illiterate lumpenintelligentsia" (1993, 294), namely, the notion that in the (post)modern world, classical concepts and distinctions have become obsolete.

THE TRIUMPH OF OBJECTIVE VALUE PLURALISM?

Let us be more specific. The discovery Gray believes has been fatal to the foundations of the Western tradition is, as he calls it, objective value pluralism, which "affirms that ultimate values are knowable, that they are many, that they often conflict and are uncombinable, and that in many such conflicts there is no overarching standard whereby their claims are rationally arbitrable; there are conflicts among the incommensurables" (1993, 291). For this insight Gray gives credit to Isaiah Berlin, who is reputed to have discovered it in pre-Romantic thinkers opposed to the rationalist monism of the Enlightenment, particularly in Vico and Herder. Whether Berlin interpreted Vico and Herder accurately might be disputed, but the general idea of objective value pluralism is clear regardless of its historical origins. What is not clear, however, is the idea's validity. What explanatory and critical power can be attributed to the thesis that certain ultimate values are incommensurable?

Let us note that the word of crucial importance here is "ultimate." The incommensurability of lower goods is not a problem, either for the Socratic founders or for anyone else. When Gray points out the need to choose "between a life devoted to intense physical pleasure, and a life devoted to long-term projects, or the life of a family man who wishes to live long enough to see his grandchildren grow" (1993, 293)—and he gives many examples of that sort—by no stretch of the imagination does he strike a deathblow at either the Greco-Roman or the Judeo-Christian tradition or at others of much importance. In the classical capitalist ethos, for example, these types of life were clearly commensurable and were evaluated hierarchically. But even if they were not, this would not make the slightest difference because it is obvious that an ethical system must have—as the ancient Greeks were the first to notice—a complex architectural structure that encompasses various hierarchies. One cannot argue that since doors and windows do not compare on a scale of importance, the project of building a house lacks unity; similarly, we cannot argue that since a culture does not possess criteria by which it can rank the value of the life of a hermit against that of a warrior, that culture is fragmented and lacks an overarching ideal. To make such a conclusion plausible Gray imputes to the classics a belief in "a single scale of excellence" (1993, 289), but such a scale, which would make it possible to compare every pair of aspects of social life, is a rather absurd notion and was never claimed by any major classical thinker. Certainly natural law, to which Gray alludes in this context, was never thought to be "a single scale of excellence."

Lower incommensurables have been a part of our experience from time immemorial, and it would be odd to think that the Greeks or the medieval Christians or Jews were somehow unable to identify them. It is also misleading to speak, in this context, of "tragic choices" (1993, 293) and to imply that the very ancients who discovered and interpreted the notion of the tragic for us—which we moderns have been incapable of reproducing or imitating—were blind to it.[1] Choosing between becoming a priest or a soldier, two clear incommensurables, is no more tragic than staying at home in the summer or going on a vacation. Indeed, if anything, it is Berlin's and Gray's objective value pluralism that seems to be devoid of the tragic in any meaningful sense of the word. Apart from the question of a religious dimension of the ultimate—an essential component of the tragic, and hardly an issue for Gray and Berlin—objective value pluralism lacks two essential ingredients for the recognition of tragedy: the notion of necessity and the notion of unity. When there is no impersonal necessity—fate or a higher moral imperative—there is no tragedy. Antigone and Creon, viewed in the light of value pluralism, are at best impractical doctrinaires, and at worst stubborn blockheads, unable to see that the only sensible solution for them was a compromise that, unaccountably, they refused to make. Similarly, there is no tragedy when there is no sense of the unity of morality, however vaguely felt. What moral loss is there for me when I become a priest instead of a soldier if they are treated as two incomparable ways of life, each having its own excellences? I would venture to maintain that moral pluralism, especially of the postmodern version, is inherently anti-tragic and was conceived as such. In a fragmented world, where there is no moral center but only peripheries, each periphery becomes its own disconnected center: So many options are regarded as equally good that few may feel degraded by alternative ways of life or alternative moral outlooks. Even the fact that some forms of life are obviously unattainable to us is hardly frustrating because, given their radical incommensurability with how we live, we do not even know what we are missing: How many American university professors or TV anchormen find it tragic that they cannot experience the joys of Eskimo life, undoubtedly valuable by some nonrelative standards?

Objective value pluralism is, by contrast, important with respect to ultimate values. Its message is crucial in constructing any ethical system that proposes to give an ultimate and exhaustive interpretation of morality. All absolutist theories thus fail in some respect because one cannot construct a system that would satisfy all human ideals—one in which people would be fully natural and fully civilized, where there would be absolute justice and absolute compassion, and so on. This is what renders utopian the tendency to try to include in one social order all that men have aspired to throughout their history. Yet there are several reasons to think that the importance of the incommensurability of ultimate values in ethics and political philosophy has no bearing on the question of the relevance to the modern world of classical philosophy.

First, it is not true that a recognition of incommensurability was alien to "the Socratic founders." Even Plato, undoubtedly the most hierarchical and absolutist thinker of antiquity, saw the inherent incommensurability of some important values. For example, in the *Theaetetus* there is a long digression about the inherent conflict between the city and the philosopher that might be interpreted as a conflict between politics and truth, civic life and contemplative life, and so on.[2] And although Plato did not have the slightest doubt as to which side was superior, the conflict still illustrates the incommensurability of values because both sides must suffer each other and neither may hope for victory (unless it be, as the trial of Socrates showed, a physical victory of the *demos*): Both politics with its imperfections and philosophy with its search for perfection are irreplaceable. In the *Politicus* we have another case of incommensurability, this time illustrated by three different hierarchies of political regimes, each according to different and mutually exclusive criteria, effectively undermining any claim to "a single scale of excellence." Particular attention is drawn to the distinction between regimes that, based on laws, are safe but imperfect, and those that, in aspiring to imitate the perfect art of politics, are not safe and are likely to degenerate into tyranny. An even more explicit example is in the *Laws*, where Plato compares "two matrices of constitutions from which all others may truly be said to be derived": monarchy and democracy (693d). These two matrices serve two antithetical values, authority and liberty, but both constitutions are good: "This was why we took the examples of the most autocratic of communities and the freest, and are now asking ourselves in which of the two public life is what it should be. We found that when we had a certain due proportionality in either case, in the one of authority, in the other of liberty, there was a maximum of well-being in both societies" (701e). A mixed constitution, which is a solution to this dilemma (an idea to be taken over and elaborated by Aristotle), does not alter the essential incompatibility of the two "matrices," because their combination is achieved through a compromise by which they lose their ultimate character. This is exactly how divergent values are combined in modern regimes. The modern Western world has succeeded in partially overcoming the conflict between liberty and equality by increasing both simultaneously; it has also succeeded in making its institutions and practices both more just and more compassionate. Even if, as some argue, we have come to a point where we cannot move farther in implementing both pairs of values and must trade more liberty and justice for more equality and compassion (i.e., social justice), or vice versa, this does not alter the fact that to a certain degree a compromise satisfactory for both parties—social democrats and libertarians—is feasible.

Second, while the Socratic founders and the medieval philosophers believed in a hierarchy of goods, the highest good about which they spoke did not have an easy application to practical matters. It was more a theological or ontological concept than a moral or political one. Plato, for example, clearly refers (*Rep.* 511b) to the supreme form of the Good in discussing how the philosopher grapples with the problem of knowing the Unconditional and the Unhypothetical (*to anypotheton*). The *Republic* was probably his only attempt to make some transition from knowledge of the absolute to knowledge of politics. In the other dialogues, however, his theological or ontological analyses did not bear obvious translation into political precepts, or if they did, they pointed to the diversity of legitimate political regimes. In Aristotle the ideal of the contemplative life in the tenth book of the *Nichomachean Ethics* also leads us to theology rather than to politics. For "such a life," Aristotle writes, "would be too high for man; for it is not in so far as he is man that he will live so, but in so far as something divine is present in him" (1177b25–30). The other interpretation of the highest good, presented in the first book and usually called inclusive because it is composed of several independently valued things, does have political implications but it does not sanction a single regime. Similarly, when Aquinas speaks of *lex aeterna*, he defines it theologically as *summa ratio in Deo existens* (*Sum. theol.* I-II, 93, 2); when he comes to *lex naturalis* and then to *lex humana*, more diversity is allowed.

Generally speaking, the fact that classical political philosophy had a theological dimension enabled its practitioners to conceive of the highest good in a noninstrumental sense and to avoid the simplistic image of "a single scale of excellence." Nothing in the concept of the highest good prohibited them from seeing the complexity of political institutions and of their evaluation. If they were too eager to establish hierarchies, it was not because of the concept of the highest good, but because they thought political equality was less valuable than we do. Naturally, the fact that the theological dimension has evaporated from large areas of modern philosophy does affect the way we assess political institutions. But this is a different problem from the alleged "end of the classical tradition" as understood by Gray.

Third, objective value pluralism is not itself immune from the error Gray wants to combat. It is not, for example, free of utopian inclinations. The fact that certain values are incommensurable and cannot be combined may have been fatal to projects of perfect government like Plato's or Campanella's, but it does not eradicate all possibility of a utopia, that is, a final pattern of a political order. The best example of such a pattern is Robert Nozick's "utopia of utopias" or "meta-utopia," as he calls it,[3] an order that potentially consists of infinitely many communities, each serving different values or combinations of values. The dilemmas of incommensurability are thus retained, though at the same time rendered powerless, because in an order of segmented pluralism all divergent ethical systems may very well coexist and all forms of life may be represented, while individuals have a chance to go at will from one to another. To avoid a possible misunderstanding, let us note that Gray is highly critical of Nozick's philosophy and for good reasons. He also openly dissociates himself from such liberal fantasies as Mill's "experiments in living," which, different as it was from Nozick's view, also implied the possibility of an unproblematic replacement of one form of life by another (1989, 243-44). Yet in these criticisms Gray does not go so far as to admit that a significant element of easy universalism—of the type he criticizes—also inheres in objective value pluralism.

The banal truth is that in modern universalistic and globalistic ideologies, far from encountering Platonic moral authoritarianism, we almost always start from the assumption of the incommensurability of values and seek to make the world safe for moral diversity. This might be, I admit, a crude version of value pluralism, but it is value pluralism nonetheless. Particularly in postmodern thought, with which Gray has some sympathy, we are promised a new era of global polycentrism—of both more individual freedom and more solidarity, of both more individual self-determination and more community, of both multipolarity and more global communication.[4] To my knowledge, there has never been a project in the history of political utopianism so deliberately planned to satisfy the requirements of incommensurability.

This pluralistic utopianism might be an important link—even if we disregard all others—between the classical and the postmodern search for perfection. Those who opt for the new world where value pluralism will be the highest principle do not differ much from the classical utopians in the confidence they display in the beneficial character of their project. They also share a sense of political and moral finality that the classical philosophers applied to omnipotent bureaucratic structures, and with which they defend a centerless order based on foundationless epistemology and serving nonhierarchical human ideals.

CIVIL SOCIETY AND *WELTANSCHAUUNG*-STATES

In the next step of his argument, Gray reasons that since universalist liberal ideology is misconceived (oddly, he does not seem to distinguish between ideology and philosophy, which results in a considerable simplification), it fails as a formula for the modern world. In addition, it might become a force threatening existing diversity, as it tends to erode inherited practices, both nonliberal and liberal. This point seems to me well taken. The homogenizing power of liberalism is, I think, a major factor penetrating deeply into modern life, and Gray is right in treating the ideology of diversity as a liberal self-deception, ultimately leading to the destruction "of our patrimony of civil institutions that is presently well under way in the West" (1993, 327).

Having rejected universalism, Gray puts forth the thesis that what we are left with, what is worth defending and what in fact represents "a near universal" idea of political order, is civil society. It is "near universal" because it is devoid of teleology and merely points to "a necessary condition, in virtually all contemporary historical contexts—which are contexts of cultural pluralism in varying degrees—of a common life for those with divergent values and conceptions of the world" (1993, 320). Civil society, in Gray's account, appears capable of embracing many forms of collective life, not only democratic but also authoritarian; many cultures, Western and otherwise; and many of the forms of social life found in different historical epochs. There is nothing inherently modern, liberal, or European about it, although it might have been a European invention.

Civil society is defined as "the domain of voluntary associations, market exchanges, and private institutions within and through which individuals having urgent conceptions and diverse and often competitive purposes may coexist in peace" (1993, 159). Its constitutive features are that: (i) "one of its contraries" are the "*Weltanschauung*-states of both ancient and modern times," meaning that "a civil society is one which is tolerant of the diversity of views, religious and political"; (ii) it requires that "both government and its subjects are constrained in their conduct by *a rule of law*"; and (iii) its central institution is "the institution of private or several property" (1993, 314–15).

This part of the argument is largely convincing, though far too laconic, considering the complexity of the issues. Yet here, too, some objections can be raised. I will leave aside the questions whether the distinction between the "universality" Gray rejects and the "near-universality" he es-pouses is sufficiently well qualified to hold, and whether what he dis-misses as groundless universalism might not be reformulated in condi-tional terms, that is, in the very way he defines "near-universalism." To discuss this would require a detailed analysis of specific theories drawn from classical philosophy (the Socratic theory of the unity of virtues, for example) and would go well beyond the limits of this essay.

The weakest part of Gray's reasoning about civil society is, I think, the first point, contrasting civil society with *Weltanschauung*-states. In its posi-tive formulation it becomes almost circular or, depending on how one looks at it, tautological. The statement that "a civil society . . . is tolerant of the di-versity of views"—which is supposed to give us one of three features of civil society, the other two being the rule of law and private property—sounds like a definition of it ("individuals having urgent conceptions and diverse . . . competitive purposes may coexist in peace") and is therefore superfluous. The negative contrast with *Weltanschauung*-states is thus obvi-ously preferable. The problem is of course the meaning of the German term, which, surprisingly, Gray never explains. His illustrations—communist to-talitarianism with its quasi-religious ideology, theocratic regimes, and a hy-pothetical American society in which liberalism becomes a ruling ideology in the way Marxism was in the Soviet Union—are hardly informative: first, because *Weltanschauung* denotes something less rigid and less easy to artic-ulate in the form of an ideology than it is in these examples, being more a common culture than a codified doctrine; and second, because these are ex-treme cases. Are we to suppose that there is no civil society unless common culture is abandoned or ceases to play any role in political life? If so, most Western polities would not count as having strong civil societies: Can one not say that France or Britain or Japan or the United States each possesses a type of cultural identity that is reflected, however imperfectly, in its polit-ical institutions, that each of those states serves, and is partly determined by, a certain historically farmed *Weltanschauung?* Between commissars and ayatollahs on the one hand, and no common culture on the other, there is a long way; there are many shades of *Weltanschauungen.* How do they stand in relation to civil society? Most Christian societies, to give an obvious ex-ample, were clearly *Weltanschauung*-societies, but Gray would certainly in-clude them among social orders characterized by strong civil societies; the same goes for the modern Israeli society.

A note of bewilderment might be added to these complaints about im-precision when one considers other statements about the relationship be-tween culture and politics that are difficult to reconcile. In Gray's essay "The Politics of Cultural Diversity," he challenges the idea that "the vari-eties of human identity . . . ought nevertheless to be mirrored or imprinted in the central institutions of political order" (1993, 254), suggesting that, in his view, political institutions should be culturally neutral. On the other hand, in his piece on Oakeshott, he makes a contrary statement:

> It may well be that it is precisely in its kinship with classical liberalism on the nature of the authority of the state that the Achilles heel of Oakeshott's political thought lies. Both assert that the authority of a modern state depends neither on its success in any substantive purpose nor on its relationship with the cultural identity of its subjects. . . . For us, who live in an age of mass migrations and fundamentalist convulsions, and who are witness of the dependency of political allegiances on resurgent local cultural identities, ethnic and religious, in the post-Communist world, it is clear that the authority of the state that . . . acts as a custodian of civil association . . . cannot long do without the support given it by a common culture. (1993, 45)

The problem of *Weltanschauung* and politics, of common culture and institutions, is particularly relevant to premodern and nonliberal civil societies, which Gray rehabilitates and rescues from the moral anathema put on them by liberal ideology. (Let us suspend, for a moment, the question of whether and to what degree a modern liberal civil society needs a common culture.) It seems rather obvious that in premodern societies political institutions drew their strength more from culture in the broad sense—religion, moral, and institutional traditions, strong group loyalty (as in the case of the Polish gentry, which built its own historical mythology)—than from coercion, which was fairly inefficient compared to the coercion in modern totalitarian countries, or from such abstract notions as utility or contract (which are more characteristic of modern societies, mobile and abstract). Gray is, needless to say, aware of all this, yet occasionally he seems to forget it:

> On the view presented here, civil societies, in all their legitimate varieties, are the living kernel of what was "liberalism." Even when their political institutions are authoritarian, or their moral culture not individualist, civil societies of all kinds embody a voluntarist conception of human association, and thereby express (or soon come to animated by) a culture of liberty—a culture in which individuals are free to come together in pursuit of shared purposes, but need have no enterprise in common. (1993, 318)

While authoritarianism and liberty are obviously combinable, as in Hobbes (though Gray's term "culture of liberty" is, in my opinion, inappropriate in this context), I find it hard to understand how a nonindividualist moral culture can embody "a voluntarist conception of human association." The whole point of nonindividualist moral culture is that institutions and associations are not man-made conventions but corporate persons which have, so to speak, lives of their own, to which individuals have obligations, to which allegiance is seldom voluntary, and from which exit is certainly not a matter of free individual decision.

POSTMODERN LIBERAL MAN IN
LIBERAL CONSERVATIVE SOCIETY?

The final step in Gray's argument is his conception of modern liberal civil society, which he believes to be a viable alternative to the type of order that is proposed by liberal ideologies. This society is simply a complex structure of liberal practices and institutions, historically singular and ultimately contingent, which we have inherited and which is our fate. It does not derive from timeless truths about human nature, morality, or the essence of being, and there is no philosophical argument that can make it universally binding or historically necessary. It does not exist through abstract principles but through our participation in the inherited institutions and forms of conduct which, in turn, give us information about what we are as a community, what it is legitimate to aim at and with what means. All liberal slogans such as liberty, equality, or progress make sense only as practices rooted in our cultural legacy and in the experience this legacy conveys.

This description, as it is easy to see, contains tenets that go back to Edmund Burke and that were later to recur in many versions of the British liberal-conservative tradition. But what is new in Gray is what he adds to this description and how he characterizes the people and ideas that keep this society going. It is the combination of these two elements that produces Gray's postmodern liberal conservatism.

First, he rejects the communitarian notion of "a radically situated self" and its implication that an individual is defined by membership in a single moral community. In the postmodern world we are shaped by a different kind of experience:

> The experience of marginality is familiar to all of us as a dimension of our identity which is integral to it. Because it is our condition to belong to many different, and often discrepant networks and communities, we belong wholly to none of them. The power of distancing ourselves from any relationship or attachment, of imagining ourselves to have severed or altered any one of the many involvements which enter into our identities, is itself a central element of our identity. (1993, 263)

Second, Gray's moral theory is built around a concept of "human flourishing" and is supported by an epistemology he calls internal realism. "It specifies as the subject matter of ethics human well-being and flourishing, not as consisting merely or mainly in subjective preferences or desires, but as a matter that is at least partly objective, encompassing the use of human capacities in a life that is, or may be, reflectively judged to be worthwhile" (1993, 295). But can we speak of the objectivity of values when postmodern individuals, shaped by the experience of marginality, no longer treat any moral commitment to a community as irrevocable? Gray explains: "Values . . . are discovered by us when we find our responses coming to equilibrium under appropriate circumstances of experience and reflection. Such realism is a form of *internal* realism, in that it conceives of values or reasons for action, not as external Platonistic entities of some sort, but as truths about our natures and practices" (1993, 297).

Third, Gray posits his own conception of the person—compatible, as one would expect, with a rejection of a radically situated self and with his notion of internal realism. In this he acknowledges inspirations from Hobbes, Hume, and Spinoza:

In Hobbes's model the person is equipped with desires and goals and with the disposition to prevail over others in contexts of material and moral scarcity. He is not a creature altogether devoid of moral attributes, since he has the capacity to make and keep promises, but he is not defined by any ideal. . . . The person, possessing this autonomy of Humean rather than Kantian kind, will have reason to be prudent if and only if, prudence is dictated by his goals. . . . If we want a formula for the conception of the person, we may turn from Hobbes to Spinoza, and equip our construction with the attribute of *conatus*—the disposition to assert one's power and freedom in the world. (1989, 181–82)

In view of all this, the question of fundamental importance becomes, obviously, what type of consensus can be formed among such persons, each seeking internal reflective equilibrium and each asserting in action his power and freedom. Gray writes, for instance, in a discussion of Rawls's recent work, that

undergirding our experience of moral diversity and conflict, our culture contains a subterranean layer of convergence on how persons are to be conceived as moral beings. . . . Our society does harbour value-perspectives and views of the world that are incommensurable and, despite this . . . we do appear to be animated by a shared sense of ourselves as individuals. . . . [Yet] it is far from clear that an investigation of our cultural tradition in its contemporary manifestations would yield much in the way of a shared conception of the self. . . . I cannot see that overlapping consensus has any definite content—unless it be only the minimal sense of self, or individuality, that is preserved across conflicting commitments and forms of life. (1993, 180–81)

In another passage, characterizing his own "postmodern liberal conservatism," Gray writes:

What is important is the possibility of a form of political solidarity that does not depend on shared moral community, but only on the mutual recognition of civilized men and women. Such solidarity may be . . . as rare as it is precious. . . . Yet, so long as we can learn the skill of defending with inflexible resolution an order we know to be underwritten neither by nature or history, we have reason to hope that the idea of a society of many distinct but inter-penetrating traditions, a society in which men and women come to respect and cherish their differences and are ready to act together and protect them, is more than an idle dream. (1993, 271)

In yet another passage, in which Gray explains his objective pluralist epistemology, he writes that

though convergence is expected on judgements as to which forms of life em-body human flourishing and which do not, there will not be convergence as to which among these is to be adopted, since the conceptions of the good they express are incommensurables. Further, within any conception of the good or the form of life it animates, there will be convergence on its compo-nent goods and excellences; but not on what is to be done when they come into conflict with one another. (1993, 312)

I have quoted extensively from Gray's books to demonstrate how ram-ified his conception is and how many different fields it covers. One point, however, seems obvious at the outset. Considering the fact that in the quoted passages we find most of the important pieces of information that the books contain on this subject, Gray's exposition appears much too synthetic in view of the complexity of the problem he has undertaken to analyze. A case in point is Gray's epistemology, a vital aspect of his inter-pretation of civil society, which also underlies the notion of human flour-ishing. Here, however, disappointments await us. The statement about values as "responses coming to equilibrium under appropriate circum-stances of experience and reflection" does not say much, lacks clarity, and poses too many questions (almost every word needs explanation) to pass for a plausible epistemological hypothesis. The same method of laconic presentation may be held responsible for certain incongruities of which Gray's conception is unfortunately not free. A good example is provided by the three views just quoted about the nature of the consensus in a lib-eral civil society. The first quotation allows that there is virtually no con-vergence in terms of moral content, so that the only common idea is indi-vidualism, understood as a shared conviction that human individuals are moral agents. The second quotation holds that an order animated by such a thin consensus on individualism may generate a "solidarity of civilized men and women" and be defended "with inflexible resolution," which is a somewhat bold conclusion considering the shallowness of what binds people together. The third quotation, claiming that in a liberal civil soci-ety we may hope for a consensus about "which forms of life embody hu-man flourishing and which do not," clearly contradicts the first passage, which said that the consensus does not have "any definite content."

The incongruities are, I think, deep and stem from the basic problem that pervades Gray's entire conception: a disjuncture between a thick interpretation of society and a thin interpretation of human nature and morality.

In many respects modern civil society resembles, in Gray's view, premodern civil societies, having a comparable variety of institutions and practices as well as a rich network of group loyalties. Gray seems to argue that underneath a veneer of universalist ideologies, such as communism and liberalism, one finds richly diversified social structures, respected as our heritage but at the same time subject to alterations. Even the postcommunist countries have, he claims, their own original forms of civil society that have come to the fore after the abolition of the ideocratic system, which was originally imposed on them, he persistently repeats, through the idiom of Western ideological universalism. He speaks of modern civil society as "a society of distinct but interpenetrating traditions" (1993, 271); he believes it has to have "a rich public culture containing a diversity of worthwhile options" and "a rich cultural environment," and for this reason he attaches particular importance to the category of "form of life," maintaining that these "are intrinsically valuable activities or practices, independently of the contribution they make to the good lives of individuals," and that "it is they, not the individual lives in which they are instantiated, that are ultimately and primordially valuable" (1993, 309).

It thus comes as no surprise when Gray asserts that "individualism is never the bottom line in what has value" (1993, 311), by which he means that individual preferences are not the ultimate standards but that individuals may flourish only through the "forms of life"—art, science, politics, family, and so forth—that social practices have generated and perfected. The obvious implication is that the richer a society is in forms of life, the more opportunities it allows for human flourishing. Let us also add that this thick conception of society is strengthened by Gray's notion of philosophy, or rather "theorizing," his preferred term. Philosophy is, in a way, subservient to practice: Its task is to illuminate the world of practice from within. Societies develop through their own logic and dynamic, and philosophy cannot be their guide, nor their guardian.

Gray is not unaware of all the processes that might undermine society as he wants it to be, particularly the self-destructive processes that are generated by liberal civil society itself. In *Liberalisms*, for example, he notes somewhat en passant that "a liberal order undermines important virtues, including virtues upon which that order itself depends. The hedonism characteristic of market societies may threaten the martial virtues that are indispensable to it, and individualism may weaken the familial virtues on which an individual order rests" (1989, 260–61). Yet remarks of this type are rare, and usually in the context of arguments directed against the hubristic assumption of liberal ideology that the society it upholds is self-sufficient and superior to all nonliberal ones. The general impression one derives from Gray's work is, in contrast, that liberal civil society has preserved its internal richness and complexity and that there are no tendencies in modern culture powerful enough to make us doubt that it will continue to do so, apart from the threat posed by liberal ideology. Since he leaves out such obvious homogenizing factors as technology and virtually ignores the impact of liberal practice—which may be no less homogenizing than that of liberal ideology—Gray's conception sometimes appears almost aprioristic: It is a definition of civil society, not a diagnosis of modern liberal reality, that stands behind his picture of thriving heterogeneity.

To what extent this picture is defensible is of course a debatable point, but what matters here is that Gray combines—unacceptably, to my mind—this picture of a society with a thin interpretation of the human person. This is a person, it will be recalled, whose sensibility is largely liberal and postmodern, shaped by an experience of marginality; a person who thinks and acts according to certain cultural codes, fully aware of their ultimate foundationlessness; a person who, belonging to many communities, "belongs wholly to none of them"; one who can distance himself "from any attachment" and has "the power of imagining himself to have altered any one of the many involvements which enter into his identity"; one who resembles a Hobbesian man whose moral attributes do not go beyond "a capacity to make and keep promises," but who shares with other members of the community the belief that some forms of life are more valuable than others; one who "has reason to be prudent if, and only if, prudence is dictated by his goals"; one who "is not defined by any ideal" but by "the disposition to assert his power and freedom," yet one for which this disposition is curbed by culturally conditioned "internal realism."

It is far from clear how this person—coming as close to the Weberian notion of *Entzauberung* (disenchantment) as one can imagine—relates to Gray's society. My opinion is that Gray commits a mistake that is not rare in those political theories that acknowledge their philosophical debt, however qualified, to postmodernism. He assumes that someone who sees through the abstractions that have allegedly mystified human existence for ages and who no longer finds much credibility in Logos, Nature, Essence, Moral Order, Telos, and other such categories that have traditionally shaped our mind and its reading of reality, will somehow refrain from using his deconstructive razor in the world of inherited practices and traditions; that a person whose mind and heart have become disenchanted will cherish and defend the element of enchantment that inherited practices and traditions must have in order to persist; that, for this person, there will still be such a thing as "many distinct but interpenetrating traditions" and indeed that the term "tradition" will mean, despite the experience of *Entzauberung*, something more than a Hobbesian modus vivendi or a set of epistemological conventions. What and who, one might ask, will keep those traditions, forms of life, and practices alive if no one holds any serious attachment to any one of them, and if everyone can at every moment distance himself from, and imagine himself to be free of, any involvement in them? Can a society have "a rich cultural environment" in the sense of a multiplicity of valuable ideals if the identity of people who live there and who create this environment is determined by "the experience of marginality"? Why should forms of life be viewed as carriers of values by Gray's postmodern liberal individual, and why should they be respected and protected "independently of the contributions they make to the life of individuals," if what primarily characterizes this individual is "the disposition to assert his power and freedom in the world"?

One might rather think it more plausible that Gray's postmodern liberal man is a cultural parasite who thrives on the environment created by others, and that his marginality, his lack of durable attachment, his individual self-assertiveness, his disenchanted attitude to ideals and collectives, exhaust inherited practices, forms of life, and traditions rather than giving them a new impetus. The diversity he publicly espouses and carries as a *Weltanschauung* emblem is ideological, not cultural. He is not a person of many cultures, and his world is not that of many cultures either. He can write on his banners the slogans of polycentrism, but he is indistinguishable from his neighbor who carries the same banner with the same slogans. The society consisting solely of postmodern liberal individuals would probably hail diversity as did no other society in history and would probably produce the noisiest ideology about how human beings flourish when "suckling on the milk of many nurses," and yet it would be a conspicuously homogeneous society. With philosophy being absorbed by liberal democracy (Rorty) or by liberal practices (Gray), such individuals will share, to use Rorty's expression, "the air of light-minded aestheticism"[5] in their approach to history, philosophy, religion, art, tradition, community, and thereby preclude the emergence of any substantial differences on any important questions. Moreover, such an attitude precludes the emergence of such differences not because they have been settled and some deeper consensus has been established, nor because individuals and groups have found some practical means of coexistence despite philosophical divergences, but because the questions themselves have been invalidated by the postmodern mind, which, to put it crudely, has become bored with them.

For some reason Gray ignores or at least does not give sufficient attention to the powerful process of homogenization which the postmodern mentality brings about. Not only is this a serious drawback in his argument, it also gives his conception of postmodern liberal conservatism such a degree of inconsistency that it is doubtful whether its two basic components—British liberal conservatism and postmodern liberalism—will ever coalesce. It is more likely that either one or the other is eventually bound to take the upper hand. One may accept a thick interpretation of society such that inherited practices and forms of life are viewed, in a way, as "Platonistic entities which exist independently of their practitioners" (1993, 310). In that case, such practices and forms of life are respected and protected as carriers of values and as important sources of individual and collective identities, and—despite the conflicts which occasionally have to arise between those practices and individual interests and aspirations—they are kept alive by the loyalty and obligation that individuals naturally have to them. Such inherited practices and forms are neither substitutes for metaphysics and political philosophy, nor are they the horizons of our epistemology, but rather are the forms of experience in which essential philosophical questions are reflected.

Alternatively, one accepts a thin interpretation of man, and society loses its cultural heterogeneity, while turning into a network of more or less effective contractual relations, conventions, utilitarian devices, and other forms of modus vivendi. Then there is no essential conflict between individuals and the forms of modus vivendi because those forms do not have an ultimate value and are by definition adaptable by and subservient to the needs of individuals and groups. Differences, no longer viewed as opposites and no longer having any metaphysical foundations, become reduced to playfulness, games, speech acts, rhetoric, rules of discourse, and so forth. To believe, however, as Gray does, that one can simultaneously have both socially entrenched forms of life regarded as values and postmodern liberal individuals who view all hierarchies and determinacies of those forms through the perspective of the disenchantment; to believe that inherited practices do not "license the wanton sacrifice of individual well-being for the collective good" (but what of nonwanton sacrifice?) and that there is not "any general conflict between [an individual's] well-being and his form of life" (ibid.)—such beliefs seem to be more like moral postulates than legitimate consequences of Gray's proposed theory or of the interpretation of current realities.

Whether the liberal conservative or the liberal postmodern approach better describes modern civil society is, of course, a different problem. Probably—and this is hardly a controversial thesis—neither should be a priori disqualified. It is doubtful, however, if one can have the best of both worlds and keep in harmony, whether in one theory or one culture, two forces that are essentially incompatible. Being a liberal conservative and being a postmodern are, to use Gray's favorite terminology, two incommensurables that cannot be combined. I still fail to understand why Gray has invested so much intellectual energy in trying to disprove this rather commonsensical thought.

NOTES

"On Postmodern Liberal Conservatism," by Ryszard Legutko, first appeared in *Critical Review* 8, no. 1 (1994): 1–22. Reprinted by permission.

1. It is symptomatic that in this context Gray mentions a sophist as an alternative to the "Socratic founders" (1989, 258–59). The sophists have recently acquired the position—for many centuries occupied by Socrates, Plato, and Aristotle—of being our spiritual fathers, because the sophists are believed to be the first thinkers who rebelled against the authoritarianism of classical philosophy just as we now do. See, for example, Stanley Fish, *Doing What Comes Naturally: Change Rhetoric, and the Practice of Theory in Literary and Legal Studies* (Durham, N.C.: Duke University Press, 1989). This pro-sophist attitude is present also in strictly historical analyses of the sophists' thought. See G. B. Kerferd, *The Sophistic Movement* (Cambridge: Cambridge University Press, 1981), and Jacqueline de Romilly, *Les grands sophistes dans l'Athènes de Pericles* (Paris: Editions de Fallois, 1988).

2. This contrast has, of course, occasioned much comment by the Straussians; see Leo Strauss, *The City and Man* (Chicago: University of Chicago Press, 1978), 50–138, and Allan Bloom, ed., *The Republic of Plato,* 2d ed. (New York: Basic Books, 1991).

3. Robert Nozick, *Anarchy, State, and Utopia* (New York: Basic Books, 1974), 309–312.

4. As examples of this, see Zygmunt Bauman. "Strangers: The Social Construction of Universality and Particularity," *Telos* 78 (Winter 1988–89): 7–42, and G. B. Madison, "The Politics of Postmodernity," *Critical Review* 5, no. 1 (Winter 1991): 53–79.

5. Richard Rorty, "The Priority of Democracy to Philosophy," in M. D. Peterson and R. C. Vaughan. eds., *The Virginia Statute for Religious Freedom* (Cambridge: Cambridge University Press, 1988), 257–84.

5

Was Hayek an
Instrumentalist?

In a certain respect Roland Kley's *Hayek's Social and Political Thought* (Oxford: Clarendon Press, 1994) is tediously predictable. Page after page, section after section tells us that Hayek's theses are "hardly comprehensible," "implausible," and "fatally flawed," that his theory "founders," "crumbles," and "aborts," that his conclusions are "foregone," that each argument he raises is "untenable," "weak," "self-defeating." When in the concluding parts of his book Kley argues that Hayek's theory is essentially instrumentalist, one cannot help feeling that this last charge is superfluous to the overall critique; instrumentalist or not, this theory must be regarded as indefensible since all its constitutive parts have been previously demolished. The picture of Hayek's philosophy as it emerges from Kley's book is that of a gigantic intellectual failure that hardly justifies the effort to refute it.

The structure of the book, in which each chapter and subchapter, each comment on each part of Hayek's theory, is followed by a critique, is a methodological trap, constraining the author to produce rebuttals almost automatically, even when there is no obvious need for them. This compulsion to score as many points as possible is probably the major reason that many of the book's arguments are unpolished; that some are methodologically inconsistent (intrinsic ones are mixed with extrinsic, empirical with analytical, etc.); and that several are unnecessary or simply false. Those arguments that are valuable and interesting become lost in a chaotic and indiscriminate series of critical punches. Kley's study certainly has not reached the standard set by other books on Hayek written during the last twenty years.[1]

HAYEK'S EPISTEMOLOGICAL ECONOMICS

Let us illustrate Kley's method by considering his refutation of what is seen as Hayek's major insight into social theory: the epistemic role of the market. According to Hayek, the indispensability of the market is primarily epistemological: It helps to discover, utilize, and develop knowledge. To support this claim Hayek offers several arguments, of which three seem to me the most interesting. The first of these derives from economic calculation: Only the market generates the conditions in which a system of prices—a reflection of countless individual transactions—gives us reliable information about the costs and benefits involved in any economic undertaking. The second argument stems from plurality: Market society is sufficiently diversified in opportunities to create a demand for individuals' knowledge and abilities that would be ignored in a less pluralist system and that, when utilized, enrich the general pool of knowledge and open up possibilities for other individuals. The third argument is from evolutionary adaptability: In the process of history, individuals have developed abilities and gained skills, often passed from one generation to another within families and other small communities, that enabled their adaptation to the social and natural environment and constituted practical knowledge of how to handle those unique problems characteristic of a given social group or a given set of historical circumstances; the market, by dispersing authority, increases this social potential, making for greater responsiveness to reality.

The epistemic role of the market is, if I am not mistaken, the only aspect of Hayek's philosophy for which Kley has some—albeit, few—positive words to say (though ultimately these words further *reculer pour mieux sauter* tactics). The epistemological argument, he notes, "seems extremely powerful" (57); "it is . . . an original contribution of Hayek's to have demonstrated that only in markets and in a market price-system do the relative scarcities of resources and goods find expression accurately and promptly enough to make efficient production and allocation possible, thereby advancing general welfare" (199). Kley's apparent admiration for Hayek's epistemological argument extends only to the thesis that economic calculation is possible exclusively in the market. This thesis is not original to Hayek; Ludwig von Mises is usually credited with its formulation. What Hayek did was to complement Mises's argument by recognizing that economic calculation is a "discovery process, developing and spreading otherwise unavailable, latent information that is part of price formation by a multitude of economic agents."[2] Kley finds little value in the other two arguments: that the market affords more opportunities for the use of individuals' knowledge, and that it induces people to acquire and transmit adaptive skills.

The main objection Kley raises against Hayek's epistemic argument is that it "in no way goes sufficiently far to justify *liberal* institutions" (199, italics his). Before any concrete assessment of this objection is made, one cannot help noting that it seems somewhat mistargeted. It is not at all clear Hayek intended his argument to answer these notoriously difficult questions, and one may wonder whether any one argument could possibly answer them. Moreover, nothing in the epistemic function of the market would suggest direct and specific institutional conclusions rather than general guidelines; no epistemology can have such obvious practical application.

One suspects the major reason for Kley's early praise of the epistemological argument as "powerful" was to allow him to launch the following critique: If the argument is "powerful," then it should solve difficult problems. It turns out that the argument does not solve those problem—e.g., it does not tell us who should build opera houses and whether to curb pornography (60–61)—so we have to conclude that it is not so powerful after all.

On the other hand, Kley is no more satisfied when Hayek's theory permits a more specific implication. The epistemic function of the market clearly favors a great number of economic agents, which in turn strongly implies a system of private property. In that sense one can say, contrary to Kley's initial objection, that Hayek's argument "goes sufficiently far to justify" at least one liberal institution, that of private property. Yet Kley asserts that "at least in theory" markets may be grounded on other property arrangements (59). Whatever the merits of this claim, it amounts to saying that Hayek's thesis is in fact too specific in its institutional implications. At this point Kley's critique ceases to be an intrinsic assessment of Hayek's theory and becomes extrinsic: There are better theories than Hayek's, judged according to non-Hayekian criteria, such as the need for a large public sphere. This may be true, but Kley does not substantiate it with a single argument. Moreover, having conceded to Hayek that "only in markets and in a market price-system do the relative scarcities of resources and goods find expression accurately and promptly enough to make efficient production and allocation possible, thereby advancing general welfare," the *onus probandi* rests on Kley to show that a property system other than the one favored by Hayek would perform the epistemic function—Hayek's criterion—at least equally well as some theoretical alternative.

With respect to the liberal state, the other liberal institution about which Hayek's thesis allegedly fails to be sufficiently unequivocal, Kley's case fares no better. At first he mentions two specific problems about which Hayek has little to say: the limits of the consumer's freedom (the consumer may desire products, such as pornography, which are socially damaging or morally dubious), and the question of public goods. The Hayek Kley gives us could hardly have any solutions to such problems, since his epistemic argument is reduced "essentially [to] the contention that only market competition can discover the relative scarcities of resources, establish a price-system mirroring them, and thus provide the information needed for an economy efficient and sensitive to people's wants" (63). Obviously, the knowledge provided by prices cannot say anything about the importance of spending tax money on an opera house or about the damaging effects of pornography. Such judgments cannot come from the price system—and Hayek never said they could. They must stem from the rules that constitute the legal and moral order of a society.

Summing up his critique of Hayek's epistemic argument, Kley makes a more general point: "Hayek's epistemological considerations are by themselves inconclusive and do not furnish a general argument against any interventionism" (62–63). While Kley concedes that "government intervention may indeed distort the price-system," he goes on to claim that "nothing Hayek says excludes the possibility of endogenous market disturbances and informational uncertainties which only government action can abate" (62). Previously he argued that there are certain specific problems that Hayek's epistemological thesis, although "powerful," cannot solve. Now he contends that the thesis does not give us any *general* grounds against *any* interventionism. This contention not only does not follow from the claim that disturbances and uncertainties may call forth government intervention as an exceptional measure, but it is false as an interpretation of Hayek.

Hayek's epistemological argument clearly excludes the possibility that the state would *systematically* act as a corrective to the kinds of market failure Kley briefly mentions. The government cannot intervene for the sake of social welfare if this would mean tampering with the general rules of cooperation; its role is to defend those rules rather than to manipulate them in order to achieve particular ends. Here Hayek's position is in line with that of several prominent twentieth-century German liberals, particularly of the so-called Freiburg School.[3] Looked at differently, Hayek's position may be compared to a certain version of the subsidiarity principle. The primary agents are individuals, communities, and voluntary associations; if they fail, there is a possibility for a governmental action; but if the government intervenes, it is preferable that action be taken by "local authorities," which would generally offer "the next-best solution where private initiative cannot be relied upon to provide certain services and where some sort of collective action is therefore needed."[4] Kley is entitled to reject this notion of the state, but he cannot claim Hayek has little to say about governmental intervention.

FAMINE AND THE EPISTEMIC ARGUMENT

Strictly speaking, Kley has only one argument that may serve to undermine the epistemic role of the market. There are situations, he says, when
"people get the price signals wrong," which in turn might result in a drastic market failure. "Hayek never considers the possibility," Kley writes,

> that massive market changes may leave large parts of a population suddenly
> without access to the most basic goods. But, as Amartya Sen has argued, this
> is precisely what happened in various famines. People died not because the
> aggregate availability of food had fallen but because huge price shifts had
> put it above their reach. Martin Ravallion has analyzed one such case, the
> 1974 famine in Bangladesh, and concludes that the rice prices were high and
> unstable largely as a result of speculation. . . . Now, to be sure, market situa-
> tions of this sort may be exceptional in various ways. Still the example dras-
> tically demonstrates that there is more to individual adjustment than the in-
> formational side Hayek stresses. Moreover, it points to limits of adjustment,
> showing that sometimes no amount of individual flexibility will suffice to en-
> able people to link up again with the existing web of exchange relations. Fi-
> nally, it also warns against making the claim about the market's informa-
> tional capacities an article of faith. (66)

Upon inspection, there is less here than meets the eye. If the epistemological argument is indeed powerful, then one would expect an effort
to relate the market's informational capacity to the famine in
Bangladesh; in other words, one would expect an explanation of how
this particular empirical fact should make us reevaluate the analytical
assertion about the market's epistemological function. To say that "there
is more to it," and that this function should not be "an article of faith,"
is far from satisfactory.

In saying that "massive market changes may leave large parts of a population suddenly without access to the most basic goods," moreover, Kley
implies that the market may be the cause of the famine. But while there is
no doubt that the state was the sole agent responsible for the gigantic
famines in Ukraine following the Russian Revolution and in China during the Great Leap Forward, it cannot be argued that the market bears responsibility for the famine in Bangladesh. Sen and Ravaillon contend that
the market was unable to *cope with* the famine, and sometimes aggravated
it, but they do not say that the market produced it. If, as they maintain,[5]
the high price of rice in Bangladesh was the result of mistaken anticipa-
tions of future prices, it does not in any way contradict the epistemic role
of the market. Nothing in Hayek's theory would suggest that people cannot "get the price signals wrong," especially in the face of floods, political
crisis, and social upheaval. If, in a certain situation, people get the price

signals wrong, it does not necessarily follow that there is a more reliable and universally applicable instrument to get them right.

HAYEK'S INSTRUMENTALISM

To review a book like Kley's, which has no clear organizing principle, is a thankless, if not impossible, task: A thorough analysis would require that all its arguments be enumerated and given a separate assessment. Since I cannot do that, I will take up the only idea in Kley's book which, hypothetically at least, might give it a unifying structure: an instrumentalist interpretation of Hayek's thought. That such an interpretation was the intention of Kley's project we learn in the introduction. Unfortunately, in the subsequent portions of the text the concept of instrumentalism virtually disappears and does not reappear until the concluding part. There, to our surprise, we find the author saying that he had been arguing for the instrumentalist interpretation of Hayek all along (183), a claim unwarranted by the actual content of the book.

As to why Hayek's thought is instrumental, Kley explains that Hayek

> thinks liberalism is the right political doctrine because, unlike socialism and other collectivist creeds, it is committed to institutions that do take account of the social world as it is. He even deems the liberal market society the only feasible alternative because it alone admits of those self-co-ordinating mechanisms, such as the market, on which modern society vitally depends. Similarly, he portrays the institutions of the liberal market society as the work of a singular evolutionary development in the course of which they have proved their value and wisdom. So it is concerns of viability that are decisive when, in his political philosophy, Hayek endeavors to justify the institutions of the liberal market society. Feasibility considerations are characteristic of instrumental reasoning. (184)

Let us summarize Kley's argument: (a) Hayek believes that liberalism, unlike socialism, "takes into account the social world as it is"; (b) from this it follows that his main concern is the "viability" and "feasibility" of institutions; (c) such concerns are typical of instrumentalist thinking; ergo, Hayek is an instrumentalist.

I have serious doubts about this argument. First, it should be noted that (a) is very vague while (b) contains an ambiguity. Feasibility and viability are not identical; communism, to give an example, was feasible but it was certainly not viable. Consequently, (a) and (b)—if the latter is limited to feasibility—generate an extremely weak notion of instrumentalism which could be applied indiscriminately to almost any position. All social and political theories "take into account the social world as it is," in the sense that none is created with blatant indifference to what the world tells us. The whole point of controversy between Hayek and the socialists was not about taking or not taking into account the world as it is, but about what constitutes the "as it is" of the world. Even the most bizarre conceptions of the ideal human order—for instance, Plato's ideal *polis* or Fourier's phalansteries—were thought to have been derived from an accurate diagnosis of reality. All of them were considered to be feasible. At the same time one can claim with equal persuasiveness that all theories, even the most conservative ones, "take into account the world as it should be," since they reject some aspect of the status quo in the name of an optimal standard. Hayek's *Road to Serfdom*, which contained a call for a thorough reform of capitalism, is a case in point.

To improve the argument we may dispense with "feasibility" and take (b) to mean "viability," if this signifies the ability to foster "self-coordination." We would then say that an institution is viable if it is able to generate and sustain itself without the interference of an external factor, such as, for instance, a government. Socialism, according to Hayek, was not viable, that is, it did not develop the mechanisms of self-generation and self-sustenance that would have given its institutions a sufficient stability; for that reason it was bound, sooner or later, to fall apart. On this interpretation we begin to understand what Kley means by "the world as it is." Hayek—the argument would run—accepted and promoted only those institutions that, through a long process of adjustment and improvement, have become more in tune with the complexities of the world. Those that have not gone through this process—and are thus the product of a "constructivist" spirit, as Hayek would say—carry too little social experience and too little practical knowledge to withstand the pressure of reality. Viability is thus not only a technical notion—institutions that are viable are more responsive and have a longer life—but also has a metaphysical or quasi-metaphysical side to it: Viable institutions give us a better insight into the nature of the social order.

This interpretation of Hayek is congruent with a lot of what he wrote, but it has one drawback from the point of view of Kley's argument: There is little instrumentalism in it. A similar notion of viability is found in many conservative writers (such as Russell Kirk and Roger Scruton) who, while having nothing to do with instrumentalism, also favor self-generating and self-sustaining institutions that have emerged through an evolutionary process of adjustment.

There is another way to interpret the quoted passage, one that modifies the previous version. The view ignores (a) as referring to an obscure problem of social ontology. As to "feasibility" and "viability," we can use these terms interchangeably to convey loosely the simple idea that, for Hayek, a social order is "a mechanism" that, by definition, should be judged by whether it functions properly, where "properly" denotes efficient coordination. Thus, when asked why he prefers some social and economic arrangements to others—capitalism to socialism, for example—Hayek would answer that capitalism provides a better system for coordinating political and economic agents. I believe this explanation is closest to Kley's intention, though as noted, it does not seem to be entirely consistent with the text. In the quoted passage we are told that Hayek believed in an evolutionary process that gives a mechanism "value and wisdom." If so, one might say that he was not a strict instrumentalist, because he also relied on noninstrumental notions. Referring to "value" and "wisdom" presupposes that Hayek's order is not only operationally efficient, but that this efficiency is subservient to the good it produces (leaving aside the question what this good, i.e., this value and wisdom, might be). As other passages in the book show, Kley will argue that in Hayek we can separate the notion of the market as a coordinating mechanism from the notion of cultural evolution which creates "value and wisdom" (an argument I will comment on in the last part of this chapter).

HAYEK AND THE FALL OF COMMUNISM

In order to find more in Kley's use of the category of instrumentalism one should turn to other, less ambiguous, formulations. Of the few that are available in the text, the most telling comes in the introduction. "What is, in Hayek's perspective, distinctive about liberalism is less a particular set of moral and political concerns deriving from a powerful ideal of individual liberty than its unqualified espousal of the market and its system of rules. To be a liberal is, for Hayek, a question not primarily of having the right political morality, but of possessing the correct social and economic theory and, therefore, endorsing the only effective co-ordination mechanism. Liberalism is an instrumental doctrine" (8).

Here, as in the last of the above interpretations, Hayek is said to be an instrumentalist because, for him, the superiority of the liberal order consists in its efficient mechanism of coordination. To this two more points may be added which are stated explicitly in this as well as other passages. First, in Hayek there are no "moral and political concerns" derived from some independent ethical standpoint that is irreducible to the criterion of efficiency; it would especially be a mistake to attribute to Hayek the view—typical of liberals—that the independent ethical standard for political and economic institutions is some notion of individual freedom. Second, the preoccupation with efficiency at the expense of the moral principles that underlie the value of individual freedom makes Hayek liable to an even more serious charge. He was not only an instrumentalist, but also a holist (68): What mattered to him was the evaluation of whole social systems (such as capitalism and socialism), whose efficiency could be measured by the degree to which they secure peace and prosperity.

Let me start with the last two points. They amount to a rather one-sided view of Hayek, and one that would be difficult to defend consistently. A holist attitude is there, to be sure, but Kley makes too much of it. We should not forget that until relatively recently, much free-market philosophy was formulated within the context of the East-West communism-capitalism conflict, which inevitably gave it a partly holist character. Even in Ludwig von Mises's aprioristic theory of the market, which was definitely more individualistic than Hayek's, one could find a holist tinge. Kley is of course aware of this historical circumstance, but he tends to see it as spawning simplified dichotomies that, characteristically, he dismisses with the epithet "Manichean" (4).

But a dualistic perspective need not be identical with political-economic Manicheanism, and in so far as they both overlap, it need not support the charge of instrumentalism. What the menace of the communist system induced was, indeed, a shift from conceptual nominalism in the interpretation of the market (to which capitalism based on self-interest and individualism has always been prone) to conceptual realism. Yet the latter position by no means obliges us to embrace an image of capitalism as an efficient mechanism of coordination securing peace and prosperity, irrespective of individual freedom. Although, once we take this perspective, we are undoubtedly inclined to view capitalism as a distinct whole—and because of this holistic tendency we might be suspected of betraying its individualistic spirit—this whole is a cultural entity, the civilization of freedom, whose essence can be best grasped in contrast with totalitarianism. Should one look for Manicheanism here, one would find it in a contrast between freedom and serfdom, rather than between efficient and inefficient mechanisms of coordination. But once we take this position, we are less, or not only, concerned with black-and-white morality (no matter how justified it might be), and more with the theoretical project of identifying and depicting the forces that have generated and sustained a free society. If that approach is holistic, so be it, but it is certainly not instrumentalist in the above-defined sense. My quarrel with Kley's view is that it makes Hayek, at best, an unself-conscious or, at worst, a dishonest thinker who wrote about the road to serfdom, the constitution of liberty, and an order of a free people but in fact meant something different, namely, the road to poverty, the constitution of prosperity, and an order of efficiently cooperating economic agents.

It may well be that with the fall of communism, the idea of the civilization of freedom has lost the conceptual and cultural distinctness it once was believed to have, so that the search for its foundations would now be carried out in a less "Manichean" way. Such a project, however, has no appeal for Kley, nor, apparently, did it ever. In a short paragraph referring to the collapse of communism, he contends that Hayek's theory has limited "explanatory relevance": The revolution in the Soviet bloc, Kley says, was primarily political; it focused on the ideas of "citizenship, public discourse, individual rights and procedural fairness," and was triggered by "the notorious discrepancies between official rhetoric and actual achievement" characteristic of Eastern European socialism (17).

Without minimizing the impact of the factors Kley mentions, we may respond that Hayek's theory was equally relevant. He was unquestionably one of the political theorists who substantially influenced Eastern European intellectuals' view of their situation and their objectives during the last decade of communism. He made them realize that the error of the ruling system was not a poor implementation of noble ideals. Hence "the notorious discrepancies between official rhetoric and actual achievement" came to matter less than the perception that the whole rationale of the social, political, and economic order under which they lived was essentially flawed. In other words, communism came to be thought "unnatural" because it was an ill-conceived, artificially constructed system that, from its inception, had been aimed against the form of social existence that generated the institutions of freedom. The categories of "spontaneous development" and "constructivism" not only helped articulate social experience, but led to a reassessment of the place that capitalism and socialism occupied in the Western tradition. From that moment on, freedom was no longer primarily a political postulate expressed in the rhetoric of liberation, but began to be viewed in terms of a larger legal and economic order based on a moral and intellectual tradition different from the one that animated the ideologies of socialism.

Besides, for some time the whole debate between the supporters of capitalism and the supporters of socialism had not been focused on the efficiency/inefficiency dichotomy for the simple reason that few socialists seriously doubted which system was superior in that respect. The standard charge Marxist and *Marxisant* circles raised against the free market was not that it did not produce wealth but that, firstly, it had become anachronistic in the light of social and cultural processes, and secondly, that it was essentially inhumane (that is, unfair, alienating, spiritually impoverishing, etc.) precisely due to its impersonal, machine-like efficiency. The latter accusation had a further consequence. Whatever claims capitalism might have had to freedom, it was ultimately a failure: A man living in an unfair, alienating, and spiritually impoverishing society did not have real freedom. He was believed to be eager to trade what freedom he had for more meaningful values that a more humane system could provide.

Hayek challenged both of the above assertions. He dismissed the alleged anachronism of capitalism by positing a model of evolution that did not make socialism a more advanced, let alone an inevitable stage of social development. And he rebuilt capitalism's ethical foundation by reasserting what its adversaries persistently denied or minimized: that this system lives on and produces freedom, and that this freedom—criticized by Marxists as merely negative and largely illusory—should not be traded for supposedly more meaningful values, because it is a constitutive element of the whole order. By making those two assertions Hayek put the ideologues of socialism on the defensive: He made them appear, within the framework of his theory, out of tune with the times and unable to cope with the complexities of the modern world. Although this defect expressed itself in socialism's inherent inefficiency, it was a by-product of something more basic—a misinterpretation of reality (here Kley's "the world as it is" formula might have some relevance). Similarly, on the ethical side one could argue that socialism's inefficiency stemmed from its suppression of freedom, which is the fundamental source of human creativity and the condition of meaningful existence. *Toutes proportions gardées*, one could make an analogous argument against slavery: It is inefficient not only and not primarily because of an organizational failure—this might be at least partly redressed—but because it misinterprets the nature of social order and is therefore unable to withstand the pressure of change, and because it is ethically wrong in its depriving people of freedom.

EVOLUTIONISM AND INSTRUMENTALISM

To reinforce his view that Hayek was interested in the efficiency of the *mechanism* and nothing more, with freedom playing a subservient role, Kley suggests the following interpretation. Hayek, he says, proposes two separate arguments: traditionalist and proceduralist. According to the first one, "the institutions of the liberal market society—being long-standing traditions of evolutionary origin—are indispensable for the survival of mankind even though a rational justification explaining what precisely their contribution consists in cannot be given"; according to the second one, "the institutional framework of the liberal market society and self-co-ordination in the market" are indispensable because "they alone are capable of dealing with certain circumstances of modern social life in a way that secures general prosperity and social peace" (185).

In Kley's view both arguments are essentially instrumentalist, which again is somewhat puzzling. Whereas one can easily attribute instrumentalism to the second argument—the market may indeed be conceived as a set of procedures of economic cooperation whose efficiency is measured by the degree to which it secures prosperity (however doubtful it is that this was Hayek's view)—but one should hesitate to characterize the first argument as instrumentalist. Traditionalism requires that people feel attached to their historically rooted institutions and practices, regardless of whether these serve any rationally identifiable purpose, and quite regardless of whether they secure prosperity, peace, or even personal happiness.

Kley explains why Hayek's traditionalism is instrumentalist in the course of a long and complicated argument that I have been unable to put into a coherent whole. Here are some of the points he makes:

(i) "The contours" of Hayek's instrumentalist traditionalism are, says Kley, the following. Hayek's "strategy is to identify an end shared also by the adversaries of the market and to show that only market traditions, but no alternative institutional arrangements, are capable of achieving it." This common end is "the preservation of mankind and the elimination of famine and poverty. . . . Since everybody endorses the end, everybody must also endorse the only effective means to that end: the rules and institutions of the market" (186).

To this one might reply that what Hayek proposes here is not the justification of the market institutions but an ad hominem argument against socialists. Since those socialists who envisaged capitalism as a self-destructive and economically polarizing mechanism would agree that the preservation of mankind and the abolition of poverty are essential criteria for evaluating institutional arrangements, Hayek naturally presses them on this point. The actual performance of the socialist economies, in contrast with the achievements of the capitalist economies, provides an argument too tempting not to be raised by market advocates; in fact it is used by most if not all free marketeers, regardless of their possible instrumentalist tendencies. The criteria involved are minimalist and largely negative. One cannot hope to justify capitalism solely on the grounds that people living under it do not die of hunger and do not destroy one another. This may, however, turn out to be a powerful argument against those who, like some socialists, promised to achieve much more but were unable to attain even this.

(ii) Kley maintains that Hayek's defense of the market is irrational and can be made rational only on instrumentalist grounds. He recapitulates Hayek's notion of his conceptual antagonist, "constructivism," which he characterizes by three tenets: (a) "all social institutions are, and ought to be, the product of deliberate design"; (b) "reason is sufficiently powerful to know, and simultaneously to take into account, all the details of the human conditions necessary to shape the institutions of society according to the preferences of its members"; (c) "all institutions not visibly serving approved ends . . . should be discarded," a tenet Kley calls "explanatory explicitness" (187–88). Kley makes two points about this last tenet: first, that Hayek, in rejecting the possibility of an explicit argument in favor of the market, in fact rejects any possibility of justification, rendering his defense of the market "a truly irrational undertaking and a pointless endeavor" that can only issue in "quietism and blind submission" (189); second, that "to maintain, against the constructivist maxim of accepting only what one *understands*, that we have never been able to comprehend moral rules *in the sense in which we understand how the things that we manufacture function* is to share with constructivism the idea that in principle, if one had the knowledge, moral rules could be understood analogously to how manufactured things work" (190).

The first two tenets of constructivism Kley leaves without comment, which may indicate he, too, finds them objectionable. This is not a far-fetched conclusion, since they are extremely bold and easily challenged: There are institutions which are not the products of deliberate design, and reason cannot be sufficiently powerful to master all factors that make a good institution. Once we agree on that, we may find the notion of explanatory explicitness suspect and sympathize with Hayek's idea of the social process as the accumutation of practical wisdom, irreducible to explicit formulae. To have confidence in this accumulated knowledge and, consequently, in the institutions credited with carrying it need not be irrational; in fact, what would be irrational would be to search for explicit justifications after having rejected (a) and (b). Similarly, since explicit justification may not be possible, it would be unreasonable to claim that whenever it is impossible we are faced with "blind submission." This charge itself may arise only from the constructivist position, for which there is a sharp dichotomy between rational explicit argument and thoughtless quietism. Hayek's point is precisely that such a dichotomy is untenable.

This also undermines the last part of Kley's argument, which seems somewhat bizarre. The fact that one attacks the constructivists on the ground that contrary to their claim, "we have never been able to comprehend moral rules *in the sense in which we understand how the things that we manufacture function*" does not imply that by launching that attack we unwittingly share the constructivist principle that "if one had the knowledge, moral rules could be understood analogously to how manufactured things work." Given that Hayek equates constructivism with a Cartesian epistemology that deduces a chain of logical consequences from absolute, self-evident first principles, one could make a similar argument to prove that Hayek is a crypto-Cartesian: Whatever we know about our moral rules and social institutions is not knowledge that accords with Cartesian epistemology, but if we had the knowledge about those rules and institutions it would certainly be of the Cartesian type.

(iii) Kley argues that Hayek's evolutionism cannot give permanent sanction to liberalism and liberal institutions, because evolution is by definition an open-ended process. "Whatever direction institutional change takes, that theory can only note it and explain its occurrence as an increase in societal adaptiveness. It must trace liberal values and institutions back to a certain momentary environmental constellation which, if it changes, gives way to new values and institutions. From an evolutionist viewpoint, there is nothing special about liberalism" (192).

This is, I think, the strongest part of Kley's counterargument. The only reply one can make in Hayek's defense is that the criticism illustrates not a weakness of the concept of adaptiveness (and indirectly of instrumentalism), but of evolutionism. If we resort to the category of evolution and want to avoid—as Hayek does—falling into historical determinism, with its belief in the inevitability and inexorability of historical laws, we have to admit that no social or economic order deserves a permanent privileged position. And although Hayek might have argued that the transition from capitalism to socialism is not really a spontaneous one, but results from the violation of the rules of cooperation, thus deviating from the evolutionary process, this argument does not have sufficient force. While it may apply to several historical circumstances, especially in twentieth-century history, it cannot be turned into a general rule. From the strictly evolutionist perspective, the market must be seen as something transitory; at least there is no way one can rationally prevent social expectations of new and alternative institutional arrangements. Another possible defense may also be put aside. Although Hayek tried hard to avoid the trap Kley notices by conceiving of evolution as a pattern of change or a framework within which all possible developments may spontaneously occur, rather than a set of specifications of what these developments will be, he could not succeed. The pattern of change is as likely to evolve as the vision of future history.

That said, a more general comment about the interpretation of instrumentalism Kley attributes to Hayek is warranted. Apart from the fact that neither the proceduralist nor the traditionalist arguments are as instrumentalist as Kley wants them to be, his view suffers from a more serious inadequacy, which is, interestingly, indicated en passant by the author himself. "Hayek," Kley writes, "does not himself distinguish the two arguments. Perhaps, he would even have insisted that they form a coherent though complex whole" (185). This is exactly right. I would say more: The whole point of Hayek's theory, by which it stands or falls, is precisely the unity of those two arguments.

A lot of what Hayek wrote was determined by the classical problem, going back as far as antiquity, of how to reconcile two apparently irreconcilable aspects of human behavior: freedom and order. His proceduralist argument, as I understand it, is responsible for the freedom part of his message: By concentrating on procedures Hayek avoids any commitment to rigid hierarchies of ends, leaving their choice to free agents acting within a framework of rules that constitute the Great Society. The traditionalist argument, on the other hand, is not, contrary to Kley's claim, latently instrumentalist; it is conservative. Hayek's project developed in the context of reflection on the great derailments in the modern societies—a context he shared with many of his contemporaries, haunted by the specters of Nazism and Communism, as well as by their historical antecedents—which led him to believe that the only solution is a combination of individual freedom and accumulated social wisdom. As did many others before him, he turned to the British tradition, which seemed—especially in contrast to the totalitarian regimes then at the peak of their power—a perfect illustration of freedom being reconciled with an institutional tradition. The fact that Hayek talks of freedom in the conservative idiom of inherited social practices does not, then, mean that he does not have a strong independent ethical standard, that he dilutes this standard in the impersonal forces of the market or historical processes, or that he identifies it with the social status quo. For him such freedom is the only real type, that is, the only type that has not turned into despotism or an ideological ploy.

To separate the traditionalist perspective from the proceduralist one, as Kley does, is not only to deprive Hayek of the ethical force his conception is meant to carry, it is also to disregard the tension that characterizes it. We cannot rely, Hayek says, on what we have received from the past because by pursuing our individual goals we are necessarily future-oriented; on the other hand, we are not free to think about the future solely in terms of the most effective means to realize our goals, because we ourselves are the products of the past, and this past, in the form of our cultural heritage, is the most reliable source of knowledge that we have.

Hayek clearly belongs to an important, though hard to classify, group of thinkers who tried to combine liberal and conservative ideas and are, therefore, often referred to as representing a "liberal-conservative" orientation. They did not form a school or a consistent doctrinal body; some of them were more conservative (like Burke), some more liberal (like Constant and Acton). Among Hayek's contemporaries this idea was popular among some German *ordo*-liberals, Wilhelm Röpke being the best known of them. If there is anything that all these thinkers had in common, and anything that justifies the use of the otherwise clumsy and oxymoronic "liberal-conservative" label, it is their philosophical anthropology. All of them shared a certain conception of man, without which a good deal of what they said could be dismissed as intrinsically contradictory. The liberal-conservative world they depicted was possible because it was inhabited by liberal-conservative people. Most of these thinkers pointed to the British tradition (or, to be precise, to a certain interpretation of it), with its peculiar mixture of freedom and conservatism, in order to exemplify this anthropology and the forms of social existence it entailed.

Liberal-conservative anthropology describes people in antithetical terms because it is meant to account for the antithetical concept and the antithetical phenomenon of "a discipline of freedom."[6] Hayek's human being is individualistically understood because individual innovation is, ultimately, the sole source of creativity and progress; yet he is also understood as a socially embedded being who never indulges in an adversarial attitude toward the rules that underlie the fabric of the social order. He does not believe in absolute ethics of the Platonic type that would petrify norms and institutions, yet he would consider as a major threat to the civilization of freedom such prophets of emancipation as Marx and Freud, who teach that norms and institutions are the primary vehicles of oppression. As a member of the Great Society, he no longer cherishes any allegiance to premodern communities, which he regards as the relics of the tribal instincts, but at the same time he relies on mores, social conventions, and inherited practices—tacit norms that are largely the cultural legacy of the premodern tradition, untouched by the constructivist spirit of modern rationalism.

Viewed from this perspective the proceduralist-traditionalist dichotomy presents itself not as an inconsistency—"irremediable" and "palpable," as Kley calls it (11–12)—but rather as an attempt to close within one social order and one anthropological vision the two elements without which, Hayek believed, liberal society could not exist. This anthropology may not be inconsistent, but one may well suspect it of cultural anachronism. Just as one might no longer share Hayek's vision of the clear boundaries and identifiable nature of the civilization of freedom, one might also doubt whether the liberal-conservative human beings who supposedly created it still exist in modern society. The concept of man that goes back to the venerable tradition of British moderate conservatism does not accord easily with today's cultural idiom, which concentrates more on "marginality"[7] and "modularity"[8]); and any theory that is implicitly built on such a man is bound to look anachronistic. At the same time one must recognize the limited nature of this complaint: We cannot know for certain if what looks anachronistic today may not look appealingly modern after some unpredictable tide of future history.

NOTES

"Was Hayek an Instrumentalist?" by Ryszard Legutko, first appeared in *Critical Review* 11, no. 1 (1997): 145–64. Reprinted by permission.

1. Norman P. Barry, *Hayek's Social and Economic Philosophy* (London: Macmillan, 1979); John Gray, *Hayek on Liberty* (Oxford: Blackwell, 1984); Chandran Kukathas, *Hayek and Modern Liberalism* (Oxford: Clarendon Press, 1989).

2. Anthony De Jasay, *Market Socialism: A Scrutiny* (London: Institute of Economic Affairs, 1990), 11. See also Don Lavoie, *Rivalry and Central Planning* (Cambridge: Cambridge University Press, 1985), 158–73.

3. See Viktor Vanberg, "Hayek's Legacy and the Future of Liberal Thought: Rational Liberalism vs. Evolutionary Agnosticism," *Journal des Economistes et des Etudes Humanines* 5 (1994): 454–57.

4. F. A. Hayek, *The Constitution of Liberty* (Chicago: University of Chicago Press, 1960), 263. See also his *The Political Order of a Free People*, vol. III of *Law, Legislation and Liberty* (Chicago, University of Chicago Press, 1979), 41–51.

5. Amartya Sen, *Poverty and Famines* (Oxford: Clarendon Press, 1981), 131–66; Jean Drèze and Amartya Sen, *Hunger and Public Action* (Oxford: Clarendon Press, 1989), 27–30; Martin Ravallion, *Markets and Famines* (Oxford: Clarendon Press, 1987), 1–23, 57–83.

6. *The Political Order of a Free People*, 163–65.

7. John Gray, *Post-Liberalism* (New York: Routledge, 1993), 236.

8. Ernest Gellner, *Conditions of Liberty: Civil Society and Its Rivals* (Harmmondsworth: Allan Lane, Penguin Press, 1994), 97–102.

6

+

The Free Market
in a Republic

For more than one reason, the reception of liberal ideas in the communist and postcommunist world deserves comprehensive study. The societies that have shrugged off totalitarianism and embarked on the construction of Western-style liberal orders based on a free-market economy not only constitute an important testing ground for the viability of liberal principles; the experience of the East European countries, deeply anchored in traditions which in the West have been on the wane, should also suggest the effects, positive or negative, which those traditions have on the assimilation of liberal institutions in an essentially nonliberal society. The remarks that follow do not pretend to be such a comprehensive study. They are limited to one aspect of the problem, which, if my reading of the East European scene is correct, will play an increasingly important role in this part of the world.

HAYEK AND THE ROAD FROM SERFDOM

The reception of Hayek's thought in Poland began in the late 1970s. Those who took his work seriously—and their numbers multiplied rapidly—expected to find there an answer to the question that preoccupied all anticommunist politicians and intellectuals in Poland at that time. To paraphrase Hayek's famous title, these politicians and intellectuals hoped to find a road *from* serfdom. A question with a long history in this part of the world, and not always a laudable one, once more came to the fore: What is to be done? Anticommunist East Europeans welcomed Hayek's thought not because it gave them a penetrating analysis of the processes of Western civilization, nor even because it provided a conceptual alternative to Marxist or *marxisant* interpretations of how society works. It was accepted in large circles of the political opposition because it was believed to imply a long-term strategy for the relatively painless liquidation of communism. Hayek described how a free society becomes enslaved by having wittingly accepted a sweeping plan to restructure its internal order; Polish anticommunists used Hayek's ideas to convince themselves and others that an enslaved society can become free again if more and more people reject the idea of such a sweeping plan and learn to act differently.

Hayek's thought came to Poland at the right moment. In 1980–1981, during the first Solidarity era, the interest in free-market economics, or rather in economics as such, had declined; politics had become the main issue dividing the country into the communist apparatchiks against the rest of society, more or less united in its attempt to contain the political power of the ruling minority. The imposition of martial law in December 1981 put an end to such hopes. The communist system, weakened as a result of the Solidarity movement, became strong again; the political opposition was crushed and society at large was disillusioned and intimidated.

In such circumstances the number of Hayekians increased considerably. Politics seemed dead, as the communists who had broken the social contract with Solidarity showed no intention of sharing the power given them by the Soviet army. It became clear that any attempt to mobilize society would be brutally suppressed by the government, and no responsible anticommunist politician wanted to risk a decision that would expose many people to repression, imprisonment, or something much worse.

In this atmosphere, many were attracted to the liberals' claim that political rebellion usually fails: It unnecessarily polarizes society, it brings irrational ideologies to the surface, it does not improve the material conditions of the people; usually it worsens them.[1] The nature of major political conflicts is such, the argument ran, that the two sides tend to resemble each other, which in this context meant the political opposition had more affinities—in terms of their fundamental approach to social problems, the approach which Hayek called constructivist—with the ruling communist elite than with those enemies of the system who abandoned politics. Instead of politics the liberal anticommunists concentrated on economics and argued that they were not interested in fighting with the communists but in changing the system. They maintained that the communists would never tolerate an openly adversary political force, but that there was a chance they would tolerate changes in the economic order: The gradual marketization of the economy might be in the interest of the communists, and it was necessary to convince them not only that it would not jeopardize their political control, but that it would also put off the danger of an anticommunist revolution and bring profits to individual communists themselves. In a way it was an attempt to bribe the communists by making them interested in private enterprise, which, it was hoped, would eventually make ineffective the dogmas of the centrally planned economy, the cornerstone of communist domination. The implementation of such a long-term pro-capitalist strategy would create economic conditions similar to those that exist in the West. In this way communism would lose its material basis and finally disappear. The economic reforms in China (prior to Tiananmen) were welcomed enthusiastically by many Polish liberals who viewed them as a model case.[2]

To what extent this scenario actually follows from Hayek's philosophy is of little importance. The Polish Hayekian liberals were not interested in the theoretical accuracy of their interpretation. They read Hayek rather superficially: not from the point of view of the scholar or historian of ideas, but from that of the activist whose main objective is to change the existing system. Despite this theoretical nonchalance, however, Hayek's enthusiastic reception resulted in the rehabilitation of a basic category in Hayek's thought—evolution. The Polish liberals became evolutionists and proudly labeled themselves as such at a time when the idea of a peaceful anticommunist revolution (for example, through a general strike) was being seriously contemplated by the Solidarity leadership and hoped for by millions of its members. The liberals believed that the gradual development of entrepreneurship and the increasing marketization of the economy provided more sensible alternatives because such processes, even if less spectacular, would sooner or later produce the rules of conduct Hayek saw as the pillars of a free society. The liberals, unlike other anticommunists, feared that a new democratic system generated by the successful overthrow of communism (which, I repeat, they thought highly unlikely) would be unable to reproduce the rules of just conduct that had been destroyed during the reign of communism. Thus, paradoxically, the impossibility of the quick abolition of communism was for liberals a good thing, although for obvious reasons they never explicitly admitted this. The time necessary for supplanting the centrally planned economy with a free market was to be used for creating the social infrastructure of the Polish society that would emerge after communism had withered away.

The liberal program was original, optimistic, and realistic, though of course highly controversial. Whether or not it would have worked we will never know, since history took a course almost nobody predicted. Much of the Hayekians' program was made obsolete by the quick, almost overnight liquidation of communism. Contrary to the Hayekians' and other groups' belief that the communist system would not fall in the foreseeable future, it did fall. What is more, the system fell spectacularly, like a row of dominos, across almost all of Eastern Europe. But the hardest blow for the Hayekians, as for no other anticommunist group in Poland, was the fact that the system came apart as a result of political action, that is, as a result of the method the Hayekians rejected and believed impossible as well as counterproductive. To make matters worse, the victory over communism was not only political, it was also almost instantaneous—it was, as some would be tempted to say, revolutionary or at least close to it. Thus the whole evolutionary strategy of minimizing politics suddenly became inadequate as the direct result of the *annus mirabilis* of 1989. A new plan was needed, and the question of "what is to be done" had to be raised again.

THE DECLINE OF POLISH LIBERTARIANISM

The attitude of liberalism toward political institutions has been ambiguous throughout the history of the doctrine, and Polish liberalism is no exception. On the one hand, liberals have been hostile to politics for many reasons, most of which essentially boil down to a conviction that the main current of life flows outside politics and that therefore the structures of the state should be reduced to a necessary minimum. On the other hand, the liberal state—especially when we take the perspective of those thinkers who, like Hayek, believe in the power of evolution—must be grounded in a civilization which generates decades, if not centuries, of political experience and a historical heritage of common practices. Liberal government, it might plausibly be argued, does not come about through the mere abolition of autocratic structures; if it did, it would be very easy to achieve. It also requires the elaboration of political and nonpolitical devices and forms of behavior which replace and supersede the functions of traditional or modern autocratic states. Whether remaining within the set of conditions specified by liberalism is enough to attain this end, or whether conditions lying outside the intellectual horizon of this philosophy are required, has been a subject of a long and still unfinished debate. Will the rules of the market alone secure social harmony, or should we also accept principles whose validity does not depend on market forces? In other words, do libertarian ethics suffice for the existence of a liberal society, or are some more austere moral rules also necessary? Of the latter, three are most often mentioned: religion (Protestantism, Catholicism and/or Judaism—a contention of such diverse thinkers as Max Weber, Werner Sombart, Peter Berger, Irving Kristol, Michael Novak, and others), communitarian traditions (for example, aristocratic traditions whose importance for freedom was emphasized by, among others, Edmund Burke and Alexis de Tocqueville), and the politics of republican civility (the American Founding Fathers). Each of these requires that individuals living in a liberal society should not be motivated only by self-interest and a sense of utility—the main driving forces of market processes—but that they should also obey certain religious norms, respect certain social and cultural hierarchies, and/or be responsible citizens cultivating republican virtues. These rules, it is argued, although vital for a good society, cannot be preserved by liberal ethics alone.

The presence of communism in Poland in the 1980s spared the Polish Hayekians the trouble of reflecting on the problem of the complex relations between liberalism and nonliberal sources of order. The means provided by liberalism were assumed sufficient for creating a free society and so it is enough to concentrate on economic freedoms while leaving other spheres of life to spontaneous development.

After the disappearance of communism this attitude changed—a fact of great significance, usually either ignored or found puzzling by most analysts of Eastern Europe, even those who praise the almost miraculous renaissance of free-market thought in the former Western provinces of the communist empire. Nowadays very few liberals in Poland still support the thesis that the market alone will generate Hayek's "rules of just conduct."[3] The strategy which seemed so promising under the communist ancien régime appears inadequate to conditions of freedom. Almost all the political parties which espouse the free market seem to share, to a greater or lesser degree, the conviction that a free market is not enough to create a good and stable society. All of them, while refusing to compromise on the principles of economic liberalism, attempt to enrich their visions of the new order with ideas which are, to say the least, hard to find in the doctrines of pure liberalism.

For the Hayekians this is certainly not an obvious course to take. Indeed, some voices were heard to the effect that the success of capitalism in Poland depends on promoting a consistently libertarian attitude under the new conditions. The argument ran as follows. The fall of communism offered an undreamt-of opportunity. Although the bureaucratic state—that archenemy of all liberals—has not ceased to exist, it has received a fatal blow. Thus the fall of communism in Eastern Europe has discredited all forms of authoritarianism: political, economic, cultural. The communist state, and indirectly the state *tout court*, has become ultimately and irrevocably desanctified. This fact ought to be taken advantage of by Polish liberals, who should push the process further until the free market emerges in its full potential. Under no circumstances should they stop the ongoing decomposition of the state. Thus, all talk about the insufficiency of the free market is mere talk—nothing but a new form of *étatisme* which seeks to reanimate the dying Leviathan. Instead of doing away with all authoritarian structures and ceding their prerogatives to the free initiative of individuals and groups, half-hearted liberal politicians are playing into the hands of their traditional enemy. Instead of openly and uncompromisingly advocating pure liberalism, they make compromises which are impossible to reconcile with economic libertarianism, or which at least do not lend it obvious support. The historical opportunity to build a genuinely capitalist system in Eastern Europe may thus be wasted.

This argument is often heard from Western economic libertarians visiting Poland who, delighted as they are by the disappearance of communism and the popularity of the free market, become somewhat uneasy about the allegedly statist and authoritarian inclinations of Polish liberals. Those who worry about what they consider to be the antiliberal tendencies of Polish liberals have received backing from one of the leading liberal authorities, Milton Friedman. In an interview published in a Polish political magazine he expressed similar fears, giving as a positive counterexample the development of Hong Kong, where economic freedom was the only organizing principle, to the benefit of all who have lived and worked there.[4]

True, contemporary Polish liberals use language somewhat different from that of their Western counterparts. They seem to appreciate the role of religion, particularly Roman Catholicism; they stress the importance of communitarian traditions; and finally, some of them combine their free-market sympathies with the ideals of republicanism and republican civility.[5] One might say the strategy of building a free economy in a communist regime has been replaced by a program of building a market economy in a republican state.

THE RISE OF REPUBLICAN LIBERALISM

The notion of republicanism was first introduced into contemporary Polish political discourse by the journal *Res Publica*, founded in the late 1970s as an underground publication and legalized in the mid-1980s. At present republicanism is becoming increasingly popular among the propagators of free-market thought, who in the 1980s were hostile to a democratic revolution. Nowadays they have to accept the new democratic regime, but they are not quite happy with the theory and practice of unrestrained democracy. They are no longer political authoritarians and antidemocrats, as they used to be under communism, but they seem reluctant to take the openly democratic stance that characterizes other political groups in Poland.

The importance of republicanism is, in fact, easier to establish than its definition, although it constitutes one of the oldest political traditions in the Western world, stretching from Aristotle and Cicero through Montesquieu and the Founding Fathers to such modern figures as Ernest Barker and Edward Shils. The last author gave a definition of civil politics that may shed light on republicanism: "Civil politics," wrote Shils, "are based on civility, which is the virtue of the citizen, of the man who shares responsibly in his own self-government, either as a governor or as one of the governed. Civility is compatible with other attachments to class, to religion, to profession, but it regulates them out of respect for the common good."[6] For all republicans, including Polish ones, an individual is thus not only a *Homo oeconomicus* who seeks success in the market, but also a responsible citizen who cares for, and has an understanding of, the common good. The latter category, particularly suspect in the eyes of most free marketeers, justifies politics as an honorable activity and sanctions the existence of the state, now no longer understood as a night watchman. For this reason, the greatest republicans put the notion of civic virtue at the center of their reflections by pointing out that individual or collective self-interest can never be a sufficient principle of political organization. The dangers of unlimited and disorderly democracy as well as of brutal and arbitrary dictatorship, which all republicans feared, could be averted, they believed, if a sense of moderation (Aristotle's *sophrosyne* and Montesquieu's *frugalité*) were deeply entrenched among the citizens of a republic, enabling them to come to agreements on political decisions in the light of the public good, as distinct from, and sometimes in conflict with, their individual self-interest.

According to republicans, democracy does not meet the requirements of the best regime because of what Burke called its "wild, litigious spirit," which induces politicians to make hasty and irresponsible decisions. To curb democratic excesses, republicans have usually resorted to two means. The first is the rule of law, interpreted in the Ciceronian or at least in the Hayekian sense as a set of general and abstract rules, in contrast to specific pieces of legislation produced by the democratic process in which various interest groups fight for particular privileges. This notion of law has gained ground in recent times in Poland (though of course in practice it is as difficult to implement there as elsewhere), mainly because the method of specific legislation was partly discredited by the communists, who used it to secure their control. Hostility towards arbitrary rules has also been reinforced by the idea of natural law propagated by the Catholic Church in Poland, still a powerful force in public life. The other republican way of mitigating democracy goes back to classical political philosophy, which for this purpose formulated the theory of a mixed regime where democratic structures coexist with oligarchic and aristocratic institutions. A republic is said to be a mixed regime in which democratic mechanisms are only part of the system, usually supplemented by elements of oligarchy and aristocracy. It is nowadays argued in Poland that although the free market often conflicts with democracy—a fact obvious to practically all liberals of all epochs—it need not be in sharp conflict with a republic, which separates the economic sphere and the production of wealth (oligarchy) from the political sphere, and where voting procedures and the will of the majority do not necessarily paralyze the economy, as is often the case under democracy. Republicans argue that those who want to imitate the systems of England, France, or the United States do not seem to be aware that those are in fact mixed regimes where democracy is coupled with oligarchy, monarchy, or aristocracy.[7]

IN DEFENSE OF REPUBLICANISM

Against libertarians who refuse to admit that the free market is not enough and who distrust republicanism as a form of statism, I argue that to a considerable degree an element of republicanism in the liberal movement of the post-communist world is a healthy symptom for three reasons.

The first has been already touched upon. It refers to what I consider a general weakness of modern Western liberalism: its failure to fully realize the debt it owes to nonliberal political and spiritual traditions. Liberals might criticize the political philosophy of the ancient Greeks, they might reject the unabashed statism of Roman thought, the hierarchical communitarianism of feudalism, or the authoritarianism of Christian social teaching, but these traditions played a crucial role in shaping the moral foundations of the Western political order, which are far more embedded in human reality than liberal theories would allow. Liberals, especially modern ones, tend to overestimate the break they made with all previous thought, which they too hastily associate with Throne and Altar, underestimating the wisdom which this thought conveys and the degree it has penetrated our culture. The liberal mind is, then, entangled in a paradox of which it is usually unaware: Vibrant free markets presuppose (and require for their survival) a certain set of values, institutions, and norms of conduct that liberalism incessantly undermines. A modern libertarian thus caricatures the republican view in these terms: "The legitimacy and stability of liberal regimes is parasitic on the lingering effects of a pre-capitalist or pre-liberal ethic."[8] There are nowadays few liberals who would agree with Wilhelm Röpke, a thinker of impeccable liberal credentials, that

> even if we conscientiously credit the market with certain educational influences . . . the ultimate moral support of the market economy lies outside the market. Market and competition are far from generating their moral prerequisites autonomously. This is the error of liberal immanentism. These pre-

requisites must be furnished from outside, and it is, on the contrary, the market and competition which constantly strain them, draw upon them, and consume them.[9]

The traditional liberals of Röpke's type and the conservative Hayekians (the conservatism of Hayek's thought has generally been minimized) belong clearly to a barely visible minority. The majority consists of—to quote Röpke again—"the inveterate rationalists, the hard-boiled economists, the prosaic utilitarians."[10] This majority, as I have argued elsewhere,[11] falls into distinct categories, similar to Röpke's. The first are the rationalists—Ludwig von Mises being their *maître penseur*—who regard the market as an order of reason and who deduce its principles a priori. The second category are the utilitarians—among whom I would place Milton Friedman—who claim that the market justifies itself by means of its unsurpassed fecundity. Those who populate these categories do not refer positively to any of the major spiritual and philosophical currents of Western history; they either ignore them, or at best argue that they can find a secure place within the liberal framework.[12] There is still a third category, that of the evolutionists, among whom Hayek occupies the most prominent position, who are far more open to the Western heritage. In Hayek one can even find traces of republicanism, and specifically the idea of a mixed regime; for example, in his proposal for a council of elders (gerontocracy? aristocracy?) that would serve as the guardian of common norms against the rampant particularism of modern democracy.[13] But Hayek's thought has also been subject to criticism by neoconservatives who argue that his concept of spontaneous development implies the acceptance of incidentality as an omnipresent moral factor, which not only runs against the traditional capitalist-bourgeois ethic but threatens, in the long run, to undermine all the ethical foundations of capitalism.[14] The neoconservatives claim that Hayek's capitalism, more open than that of other liberals, is still not open enough to what is of worth in nonliberal traditions (in contrast to earlier evolutionists, like Lord Acton, who were very much aware of the debt the liberal order had incurred from its predecessors and adversaries). Hayek's concessions, minor from the neoconservative perspective, are of course regarded as inadmissible by libertarians who frown at his alleged lack of faith in the self-sufficiency of liberalism.[15]

In a country like Poland there is a deeply felt need to accept the dominant "rules of just conduct" not only because they have been produced by the spontaneous process of cultural selection but because they are valid, which means that they can be related to something more substantial than the formal criteria of spontaneity. Hayek's theory cannot do justice to important areas of culture (religion being the most obvious example, as

Michael Novak and Peter Berger have noted),[16] and it fails to answer certain fundamental questions. How to justify the value hierarchies according to which political choices are made? What moral purposes may be elevated in a society and on what grounds? The idea of a spontaneous order will be of little help here because in order to find answers, we need philosophically weightier categories than are employed by Hayek's theory of spontaneous evolution. Can our philosophical curiosity and our natural desire to justify the order we live in be satisfied solely on Hayekian grounds, that is, on the knowledge that the basic rules of the system are something we merely stumbled upon, something that resulted from the social imitation of incidental individual innovations? Can all attempts to search for a larger meaning be brushed aside as, to use Hayek's expression, "primordial emotions"?

The second argument with which I propose to defend the Polish liberals' position stems from the peculiarity of the postcommunist world. Those who maintain that the fall of communism has left a void that can be filled by liberal institutions underestimate the strength of the communist legacy. In fact, the authority of Hayek himself can be used against them. They resemble one of the protagonists of the French Revolution, Abbé Sieyès, whom Hayek ridiculed for having exhorted the revolutionary assembly "to act like men just emerging from the state of nature and coming together for the purpose of signing a social contract."[17]

To an evolutionist, a program of building a laissez-faire order from scratch is absurd and has more similarities with French constructivism than with the English liberalism to which Hayek subscribes.[18] It should be self-evident that the postcommunist world is not a state of nature. The state as an omnipresent political institution may have been discredited, but the habits and the ideas that sanctioned it have not disappeared. One should not therefore imagine a Polish or a Hungarian society as "a clean slate," to used Plato's memorable expression, upon which a new order can emerge spontaneously, free of the specters of the past. A more likely scenario would be for those specters to manifest themselves with greater force than in stabilized societies that enjoy an unbroken historical record. Eastern Europe has gone through several catastrophes which virtually destroyed a sense of continuity. The political and philosophical ideas given a hearing in today's Poland and in other East European countries form a strange mixture of ideologies coming from different epochs and intellectual inspirations, some of which are most bizarre.

The criteria of spontaneous selection that have functioned in the West to civilize the major political movements and their ideological programs have not functioned here. Someone compared East European communism to a refrigerator which had frozen ideas and sentiments from an earlier period for several decades. Nowadays the fall of the system has caused a rapid defrosting of those ideas and sentiments, with many negative consequences: Some are anachronistic and out of touch with reality, not having undergone the trial-and-error self-improvement process which is natural in a normal political life. One may hope that once a spontaneous development begins, it will eventually lead to a maturation of dominant ideologies. This may be so, but it may turn out instead that the ideas that play a crucial role today will prevent the spontaneous development from happening.

In my view, not only did statist ideologies not disappear in this part of the world together with the fall of communism, they now exist in a perverted form. Eastern Europe, far from being a state of nature, is a highly political world where all the traditional Western political categories are used, but with different, largely arbitrary meanings. Let us not forget that communism has not been an offshoot of East European parochialism but derived its intellectual impetus from the mainstream of Western culture, much more so than, say, Nazism. The language of communism incorporated but distorted all the standard concepts of political thought. "Democracy" did not mean democracy, "constitution" did not mean constitution, "public interest" did not mean public interest. The result of this gigantic manipulation was that the classical language of politics ceased to perform its original function, which in turn led to a twofold reaction. On the one hand, the aversion to communism was extended to an aversion to everything this language denoted. People thus feared the state, not because of liberal arguments against the state, but because it was a communist one; thus the reality that was most often perceived behind the classical language of politics was a communist one. This in turn provoked an opposite reaction, a widespread longing for "real" democracy, "real" public interest, etc., where "real" was used in the ideological sense of something unconditionally good. In both reactions the complexity of each concept and its original meaning remained unknown. To recover the original meanings is a task as difficult as it is urgent. The worst thing to do would be to abandon the language of politics altogether in favor of building a civilization of the free market that leaves the political sphere in a state of barbarism.

The third argument is logically connected with the previous one. How can the classical political categories be rehabilitated? The conventional wisdom has it that the opening to the West and marketization will do the job. Whoever follows the intellectual tendencies of postcommunist Eastern Europe will not fail to notice the fascination with "being a part of the West," "joining the European Community," etc. Pro-Western snobbery has always been a remarkable social phenomenon in a country like Poland, and under communist rule it played the positive role of a barrier against Sovietization. But this snobbery has a negative side too, especially when the great divide separating Eastern and Western Europe has disappeared. The rapid flow of Western culture may bring—in fact, is bringing—various currents of ideas which are jointly identified as the essence of the West; thus Westernization is often confused with marketization and the spread of liberalism. This simplified vision of Western culture will of course slowly change, but its negative effects will probably prove more permanent. The problem is that the ideas which may find the easiest acceptance in Eastern Europe are those that are currently popular, which, needless to say, are not necessarily those that conduce to building a liberal order, though they themselves may be its products. Classical liberalism may often conflict with modernity (and even more so with postmodernity), but it is precisely modernity that, under the veil of liberalism, and without much resistance from liberals, is being spontaneously imported into East European countries. For a Hayekian, this need not be a welcome development.

In this context we may again refer to the authority of Hayek himself, who has been a shrewd observer of the disquieting tendencies in the modern world. At the end of the third volume of *Law, Legislation and Liberty* he specifically points to two sources of philosophical inspiration which he finds particularly inimical to the liberal order—Marx and Freud. Both disseminated ideas that subvert the general and abstract rules of just conduct without which the Great Society is inconceivable. Marxism is in Hayek's view responsible for relativism and egalitarianism, the first leading to the notion that different groups should obey different rules, the second leading to coercion and to a virtual end of spontaneous evolution. Freudianism, according to Hayek, is responsible for the rejection of all traditions of moral rules as "repressive and inhibitory."

It would not be an exaggeration to assert that much of what passes nowadays for modernity and constitutes the intellectual climate of Western culture falls within these two lines of thought. Marxism, often in diluted and cryptic forms, manifests itself in a popular notion of the conflict of "cultures"—whites against blacks, men against women, North against South. The assumption of incommensurable, untranslatable cultures has now resulted in the attempt to create a more inclusive political language. This fact is worth noting here because language has always been regarded by Hayek as an outstanding example of spontaneous order; the idea of an inclusive language is purely constructivist and as such has dealt a serious blow to Hayek's desideratum, because it has shown how deeply constructivism has penetrated the modern mind. Freudianism, also in diluted and cryptic versions, has continued to live in the modern concept of the self and of individual liberation, both of them leading to what Christopher Lasch aptly labeled "the culture of narcissism." All these trends may affect Eastern Europe more decisively than the ethics of classical liberalism, which is still deeply attached to tradition.

This argument may encounter two objections. First, it may be said that liberalism has nothing to do with Marxism and Freudianism, and that therefore one should not associate the malaise of modernity with liberal theory. Alternatively, if the argument is valid, we ought to try to base the new East European order on original liberal notions rather than flirting with the dangerously statist republican tradition. But both rejoinders can be refuted. While it is true that Marxism and Freudianism (as well as their modern counterparts) have little to do with classical liberalism, it is equally true that they can be and in fact are being expressed in a liberal idiom. Even if we leave aside the claims of those critics who, like Lasch, put all the blame on liberalism, we are still left with the fact that some basic liberal categories have been employed to substantiate the major tenets of modernity, including those indicated above. Among such categories, that of rights, unquestionably and originally liberal, has been extremely effective in advancing Marxist and Freudian ideas—relativism, egalitarianism, inclusive language, the obsessive concern with moral repression, and the like. By means of the concept of rights, whether individual or collective, modern authors and ideologues try to prove that different cultures obey different and mutually untranslatable rules of conduct, that evolution should be controlled in the name of egalitarianism, that the self is repressed by existing institutions and moral codes; the concept of rights, in short, can explain the emergence of "the culture of narcissism." To those who say Hayek was not compelled to make any concessions to Marxism and Freudianism, one can reply that he rarely used the concept of rights and that his theory of spontaneous evolution does not need it. But what is being imported to Poland on a mass scale as a result of Westernization and marketization is not the ideology of abstract and general rules of just conduct, but a Marxian-Freudian-liberal intellectual folklore in which rights justify all the above-mentioned ideas.

The philosophy of republicanism seems, then, a much more appealing alternative. Those who defend it in Poland argue that the reconstruction of classical political orthodoxy—and that is what republicanism is about—will better serve the cause of freedom than a thoughtless acceptance of what passes for liberalism today. The tradition of republicanism provided a natural environment for the emergence of Western liberalism, and there is no reason to believe Eastern Europe will better off without it. The only doubt is whether in the postcommunist world, in entirely new and unpredictable circumstances, the epoch-making task of marrying the philosophy of free enterprise with that of republicanism will be successful. But this is a completely different problem.

NOTES

"The Free Market in a Republic," by Ryszard Legutko, first appeared in *Critical Review* 5, no. 1 (1991): 37–52. Reprinted by permission.

1. For a more detailed rendition of Hayekian thought in Poland, see Andrzej Walicki, "Liberalism in Poland," *Critical Review* 2, no. 1 (Winter 1988): 8–38.

2. For a good sample of this reasoning, see a 1988 statement by Tadeusz Syryjczyk, one of the leading liberals and the future minister of the economy in Tadeusz Mazowiecki's government, on the predicted role of the anticommunist opposition in three years' time: *Res Publica* no. 9 (September 1988): 4–6.

3. Among these one should mention Stefan Kisielewski, Poland's most popular political columnist and the patriarch of Polish liberals.

4. Milton Friedman, "Prywatyzujcie, prywatyzujcie, prywatyzujcie!," *Res Publica* no. 10 (October 1990): 94–103.

5. For a concise description of Polish "Thatcherists" see Paweł Ziółek, "Polska prawica," *Więź* no. 3 (March 1991): 37–47.

6. Edward Shils, "Ideology and Civility," in *The Intellectuals and the Powers, and Other Essays* (Chicago: University of Chicago Press, 1972), 60.

7. This argument is most often raised by Cracow political philosopher Bronislaw Lagowski. For more details about Lagowski's views see Walicki, "Liberalism in Poland."

8. Stephen Macedo, *Liberal Virtues* (Oxford: Clarendon Press, 1990), 285.

9. Wilhelm Röpke, *The Humane Economy* (London: Oswald Wolff, n.d.), 126.

10. Röpke, *The Humane Economy*, xii.

11. Ryszard Legutko, *Spory o kapitalizm* (Krakow: ZNAK, 1994).

12. For a critique of this theory see my "Society as a Department Store," chapter 1 of this book.

13. F. A. Hayek, *New Studies in Philosophy, Politics, Economics and the History of Ideas* (London: Routledge and Kegan Paul, 1982), 152–62.

14. Irving Kristol, *Two Cheers for Capitalism* (New York: Basic Books, 1978), 261–63.

15. Macedo, *Liberal Virtues*, 285.

16. Michael Novak, ed., *Capitalism and Socialism: A Theological Inquiry* (Washington, D.C.: American Enterprise Institute, 1979).

17. F. A. Hayek, *The Constitution of Liberty* (Chicago: University of Chicago Press, 1960), 57.

18. Hayek, *The Constitution of Liberty*, 60-61.

7

✝

On Communist Illusion

To understand the nature of François Furet's undertaking one must start from a few explanatory remarks. His book *Le passé d'une illusion; essai sur l'idée communiste au XXe siècle* is what it says: an essay. It is not a scholarly work, historical or philosophical. It is a long, even very long, several-hundred-page analysis of the development of the communist idea. What also qualifies it as an essay are a loose way of presentation, a lot of digressions, colorful style, and a personal tone. One can add that it is a well-written essay, often brilliant, though not without defects. The author could make it more concise and should have avoided repetitions that occur every now and then.

In the title there are two more concepts beside "essay" that also require some explanation. The book is about the "communist idea," a concept which on the one hand seems too narrow, and on the other, unusually large. It is narrow because it allows Furet to remove from his analysis everything that does not belong to the category of "idea" but that unquestionably played a major role in establishing and sustaining the communist system: institutions, economy, social structures, etc. Although sometimes the author makes reference to political and social history, he consistently views communism as "an idea" or rather, as "a Great Idea." Hence the reader will not find information about, say, the dramaturgy of the Bolshevik revolution or the German-Soviet war, but he will be given minute details about the works of intellectuals, the ideological manifestoes or declarations of politicians. The book has, naturally, a French perspective: A large part of the material illustrating the author's argument is taken from the reception of the communist idea in France.

On the other hand, the category of the "communist idea" seems extremely spacious. It denotes a variety of things coming from different levels of discourse and from different types of analysis: A communist idea as expressed in the strategy of the Soviet communist party is different from a communist idea that appears in the theories of philosophers or in the visions of political prophets; those in turn are not the same as communist ideas that motivate social emotions or that are a part of social culture. Each of those ideas we assess differently and interpret by means of different conceptual instruments. Yet Furet treats them jointly, which a reader accustomed to terminological rigor might find somewhat confusing or even misleading. But in the essay, one could reply, such lack of discipline is admissible as long as it leads to nontrivial conclusions.

The last and by far the most important concept to be explained is that of "illusion." We find it in the main thesis of the book, which states that the communist idea was an illusion that had a long life and has just recently been discarded. The meaning of this thesis is explained in detail at the very beginning of the book. The Soviet regime, Furet writes, was closely "linked with the fundamental illusion whose value it continued to confirm but which it finally undermined by its own history. . . . Communism had an ambition to become a necessary element in the development of historical Reason," thus providing the idea of the "dictatorship of the proletariat" with the status of a scientific theory. This was an illusion that differed from one that results from an erroneous calculation of means and ends, as well as from one that comes from a naïve belief in a just cause; the illusion of communism gave man lost in history a sense of life and the benefit of certainty. The illusion did not have a character of a proposition that one could, resorting to an experiment, refute, strengthen, or modify, but rather it was similar to a psychological investment not unlike a religious faith which has history as its object. The illusion does not "accompany" the history of communism; it creates this history, irrespective of the course that the developments take, as a premise on which the experiment is based; it also inheres in the yoke of history itself since its predictive power is validated by the confrontation with reality. The roots of the communist illusion come from the political imagination of modern man, but in order to survive it had to evolve under the influence of circumstances."

This sounds familiar: The communist idea derived its power from the faith in the rationality of history that was to reveal itself through the interaction of social groups; it was a sort of "psychological investment" similar to a religious experience, not to be falsified by external evidence, but responding to this evidence with ever new adjustments and transforming this reality in accordance with what it treated as the criteria of rationality. This interpretation repeats various tenets that appeared in some past interpretations that attempted to explain the sources of the powerful impact the communist idea had on political movements and people's minds. But since Furet's main argument repeats what others said about an analogy between communist ideology and secular religion of history, where, one should ask, does the book's originality lie? An entirely new interpretation would be, obviously, neither possible nor convincing. What is most interesting in Furet's work is not the explanation of communist illusion, but its historical analysis.

Generally Furet's argument boils down to two theses:

I. At its roots the communist idea was generated by revolutionary zeal, and this zeal sustained its existence.
II. In the second—and in fact, the last—phase the factor that gave this idea impetus and credibility was antifascism.

Let us start with the first thesis. Furet maintains that the source of revolutionary zeal was a strong antibourgeois impulse created by a moral and political sensibility the bourgeoisie itself brought into Western culture. The bourgeois spirit had an internal conflict: It provided society with ideals and then accused itself of not being able to fulfill them. The highest of these ideals was equality. In implementing this value the bourgeoisie went as far as one could go, destroying traditional communities and hierarchies, and replacing them by individuals freed of all distinguishing qualities. We owe to the great representatives of bourgeois culture an idea that primarily and naturally we exist as individuals, and that as individuals we are equal.

On the other hand, however, by freeing people from their traditional hierarchies and communities the bourgeois spirit gave human life a dynamism it never had before. The society composed of separate individuals was a society of opportunity: Everyone could set his own objectives and attempt to attain them. The most obvious—though not the only—area in which these objectives could be attained was the free economy. A typical bourgeois was therefore thinking about his life in terms of economic advancement, production of wealth, and maximizing of welfare; these were the natural ends to turn to after having freed himself of communal and traditional bonds. But this new attitude created new divisions. In their natural existence the individuals were free; in their actual social existence they became dramatically differentiated in various respects, most importantly in respect of their wealth. The world of the free market did not tolerate equality; all those who were less able, had less luck, or could not adapt themselves to changing conditions were among the lower strata of the social hierarchy and were looked down on by those who were more successful.

The bourgeois society gave people a strong sense of equality and stimulated a passionate desire for it, but at the same time this society was being torn apart because of its inability to live up to the ideal. Hence a bourgeois culture—in spite of its unquestionable achievements in satisfying people's needs, particularly economic ones—generated a widespread feeling of hostility towards itself, made more intense by its own frustration. The bourgeois society was being opposed, attacked, and subverted in the name of the bourgeois ideal, communism being the most mature and the fullest expression of this opposition. By undermining the existing order and calling the erosion historically inevitable, it reinforced the revolutionary spirit. The better world was henceforth not only desirable but rational and necessary.

Communism, obviously, was not the only rebellion against bourgeois civilization; the other was fascism (and later Nazism). Despite evident differences (e.g., communist universalism versus Nazi nationalism) both these movements belong, according to Furet, to the same category; both vehemently opposed bourgeois institutions, capitalism, and parliamentary democracy; both intended to put an end to those forms of discrimination which were the effects of bourgeois civilization; both attempted to create new alternative institutions. The links between communism and fascism were, until a certain moment, obvious. One could find them in the declarations of politicians, but also in the works of some intellectuals who, like George Bernard Shaw, felt sympathies to both movements.

In the case of communism, revolutionary zeal was the main reason for an uncritical attitude towards the Soviet regime, irrespective of how this regime treated its citizens. There are two major interpretations of the intellectuals' support of communism. According to the first, the intellectuals were naïve idealists who were blinded to the reality of communism, to terror, purges, famine, repressions, because of their fanatical dedication to the idea of the secular salvation of humanity. According to the second interpretation, the intellectuals knew about these facts very well and accepted them. This last interpretations was eloquently articulated by a British historian George Watson in a much-discussed article published in *Encounter* in the early 1970s.

Furet does not directly refer to this controversy, but the text suggests that he found both interpretations plausible. The first one is best illustrated by H. G. Wells; the other, by George Bernard Shaw. Wells was convinced that every educated and fairly intelligent person must be a supporter of central planning; at least, he said, central planning is accepted by all members of the Royal Society. Capitalism is therefore doomed. During his conversation with Stalin, Wells went as far as to give some advice to the Soviet dictator. "Believe me, Mr. Stalin," he said, "I am more left-wing than you are." George Bernard Shaw, on the other hand, did not have any illusions about the Soviet regime and admired it for what it was: ruthless destruction of traditional institutions and practices. Stalin and his policies were for him the personifications of the reason that eliminated the capitalist order and replaced it with a new one.

In these reactions Furet found, first of all, confirmation of the "malleability of the Soviet myth," which could serve the purposes of visionaries like Wells and the advocates of ruthless politics like Shaw. The Soviet Union was loved for what it was not, i.e., for its social and political justice, and for what it was, i.e., brutal dictatorship.

Revolutionary impulse and communist infatuation could not last long, and after some time they began to lose their extreme forms, primarily as a result of the growing stabilization of the Soviet structures and of international relations. The world revolution did not break out, and there were no signs that it would. The only reality left to defend was the Soviet Union (Stalin's "socialism in one country"), whose internal and foreign policies were now being determined by practical concerns, not by the Great Idea. Communism would have lost its grip on the minds and hearts of people were it not for a new mission it espoused: antifascism, which at a certain moment became the main source of power for communist dynamics and the principal justification of Soviet policies. At this moment when the two political regimes—in spite of occasional and sometimes even deep political alliances—opposed each other, a great number of progressive politicians, intellectuals and ordinary citizens came to a conviction that the Soviet Union was the only alternative to Nazi barbarism.

The principal author of this conviction is hard to identify. On the one hand, it was Soviet ideology whenever it served the current objectives of Stalin; on the other hand, antifascism was propagated by the Western communist parties and left-wing groups because it gave them a raison d'être. In a way, the revolutionary enthusiasm also found its continuation in the ideology of antifascism: Not only was the Soviet Union burdened with the fundamental moral and political duty towards humanity, but this duty was denied to the Western states. The bourgeois governments were regarded as unable to oppose fascism, and sometimes even as drifting toward it. Finally, the idea of antifascism captured the political imagination of the communists because it turned out to be an extremely efficient instrument with which to mobilize social groups in noncommunist societies while concealing procommunist aims.

To make an argument that Furet does not make but that can be formulated on the basis of what he says, I would add that the illusion that communism is necessary to defeat fascism was a different kind of illusion than the notion that communism is historically and strategically inevitable. Although in the former one can still see a sparkle of the original revolutionary zeal, the slogan of antifascism came to the fore when the initial impulse of the Great Idea became exhausted. The mobilizing force was now the hate and fear of Nazism, and these feelings often masked the weakening dedication to the cause of the happiness of humanity in the new economic and political order. The antibourgeois rebellion in the name of economic justice and equality resulted from an illusion that was primarily philosophical, whereas antifascism had little to do with philosophy and was in fact a political deception. Those who accepted the idea of antibourgeois revolution were motivated by a sincere impulse of the heart—though often fanatical about the ultimate end and, therefore, tolerant of political crimes—while those who joined the antifascist movements were often entangled in rather ordinary mechanisms of deception, self-deception, lies, and manipulations.

The idealism of the first phase was particularly widespread among the intellectuals. They could diverge on the question of how to assess the Bolshevik revolution and the role of Lenin—some, like Karl Kautsky and Rosa Luxemburg, criticizing the final outcome of the revolution—but the ultimate goal, communism, remained sacred. Furet does not mention those intellectuals who criticized the Soviet regime yet stayed immune from the Great Idea; apparently they do not fit into the concept of illusion as he understands it. He gives examples of the intellectuals whose love for the Idea did not prevent them from making a critical assessment of the reality of postrevolutionary Russia.

He is especially appreciative of Bertrand Russell's *Bolshevism: Practice and Theory*, published in 1920. I think, however, that Furet is wrong. A favorable evaluation of this book, which is not uncommon among those who write on communism critically, is too generous and ignores its aggressive anticapitalism ("The existing capitalist system is doomed. Its injustice is so glaring that only ignorance and tradition could lead wage-earners to tolerate it.") and its ardent belief in the essential rightness of socialism ("I believe that Communism is necessary to the world, and I believe that the heroism of Russia has fired men's hopes in a way which was essential to the realization of communism in the future. Regarded as a splendid attempt, without which ultimate success would have been very improbable, Bolshevism deserves the gratitude and admiration of all the progressive part of mankind."). I would rather rate the book as an example of intellectual dogmatism than sharpness of perception. What Russell in fact objected to in Bolshevism was its "religiousness" and "Platonism," the usual bêtes noires of liberal thinkers. But he accepted its revolutionary program: "A fundamental economic reconstruction, bringing with it very far-reaching relations in ways of thinking and feeling, in philosophy and art, and private relations, seems absolutely necessary if industrialism is to become the servant of man instead if his master. In all this, I am at one with the Bolsheviks; politically, I criticize them only when their methods seem to involve a departure from their own ideals." One last quotation, from the very end of Russell's book, should dispel any illusion about its anticommunist message: "While admitting the necessity and even utility of Bolshevism in Russia I do not wish to see it spread or to encourage the adoption of its philosophy by advanced parties in the Western nations. Even under present conditions in Russia, it is possible still to feel the inspiration of the essential spirit of communism, the spirit of creative hope . . . to replace individual competition by collective action. . . . This hope is not chimerical, but it can only be realized through a more patient labor, a more objective study of facts and above all a longer propaganda [*sic*] to make the necessity of the transition obvious to the great majority of wage-earners."

It is interesting that the best known critical descriptions of the Bolsheviks' revolution and the system they built came from socialists who, like Russell, expressed qualified disappointment at the discrepancy between the communist ideal and Soviet reality. There were no analyses—or rather, no influential analyses—that rejected both the Bolshevik revolution and the whole system of ideas that animated the communist and socialist movements. To use an analogy, we can say that among the critics of the new Bolshevik order there were no Edmund Burkes who would have condemned not only the revolutionary practice but also the intellectual foundations of the revolutionary act and its ultimate goals. At any rate those who aspired to become the Burkes of the twentieth century never managed to play the role that the author of the *Reflections on the Revolution in France* played over a hundred years before.

Compared with revolutionary idealism, the slogan of antifascism marked a considerable decrease of ambition. It appealed, at best, to political pragmatism and, at worst, it turned into an ordinary deception. The revolutionary zeal took its inspiration from the Great Idea, while antifascism found outlet in vulgar propaganda such as international congresses and brigades, popular fronts, manifestoes and declarations, world councils of peace and progress, world council of churches, etc., usually inspired and financed by the Soviet Union or its proxies. Falling prey to such illusions was in a way more degrading than falling prey to the Great Idea, because it was connected with group conformity, credulity, servility, and sometimes sheer stupidity, vanity, and lust for power. The causes of this illusion were more ordinary; its effects, more pathetic.

Once we agree on that, we must also concede that the initial description of the communist illusion, quoted in the passage at the beginning of this essay, does not cover, contrary to Furet's claim, the whole history of the communist idea's impact on political thinking, but refers primarily to the first phase. Such a conclusion is not original. It suffices to recall that Czesław Miłosz's *Captive Mind*, which was written in the period of "antifascism" but contained the description of the first sense of the communist illusion (to be later called "the Hegelian bite") was received with disbelief by several critics. They (notably, Gustaw Herling-Grudziński and, later, Zbigniew Herbert) argued that the alleged infatuation with the Great Idea was never genuine, and it mystified the effectiveness of the brutality of the Soviet system: Those who served the system did not do so because of the Idea, but from cowardice, or moral pettiness, or vanity. In short, one can say that even if the revolutionary zeal and the belief in the salutary power of history were not sham, they were so entangled in the ugliness of life under communism that neither today nor ever before could one distinguish one from the other. For this reason, there is little credibility in the stories told by the framers of the "antifascist era" who explain their dedication to the system by their youthful revolutionary enthusiasm.

The fact that Furet does not analyze the difference between the communist illusions in the two phases is one of the weaknesses of his book, all the more visible because he devotes so much space to the "antifascist phase"). But this is not the only doubt I have.

Although one cannot deny the essential validity of the main thesis that the carriers of the communist idea were, first, the revolutionary zeal, and then, antifascism, the thesis has consequences that are not obvious. Even if we agree that in the antifascist illusion there remained an element of the initial illusion about the Great Idea, we still have to accept a somewhat troublesome conclusion that this Idea lost its appeal quite quickly. Certainly this loss of appeal did not occur—as the author suggests at the beginning of his book—in 1989. The disruption of the Soviet Empire was not the same as the collapse of the communist illusion in the first sense; this illusion must have ceased to exist earlier. When? Furet suggests that the actual end was the de-Stalinization carried out by Khrushchev at the Twentieth Congress of the Soviet Union Communist Party. Since the supreme leader of the Soviet Union admitted that Stalin and his regime had been guilty of great crimes, there was no reason to continue to believe in the antifascist mission of communism.

Everything that happened after the Congress Furet seems to dismiss as unimportant. Not only does he refrain from analyzing it extensively, he also writes about later developments as if they are not interesting at all, but merely consequences of the main drama that had been played before. Certainly the Twentieth Congress was a major event from the point of view of how the communist idea was perceived throughout the world. But after the Congress the system continued to exist, and the communist idea still had its followers and propagators. Can we then really say that nothing happened, from the perspective of the communist idea, during those forty-five years? Could it be that the system persisted only in its institutional forms, while the idea had died and ceased to affect the minds and lives of people? Are we to believe that during those forty-five years between the Twentieth Congress and the *annus mirabilis* of 1989 there were no processes that continued to invalidate "the psychological invest-ment" and that what we had in 1989 was only a revolution in political in-stitutions and structures of power? Are we to accept the presupposition that after "antifascism" there appeared no ideologies or sentiments that could sustain the attractiveness of communism?

To all these questions one can give an answer unequivocally support-ing Furet's opinion about the death of communism coinciding roughly with the death of the World's Greatest Linguist (as Stalin was called in So-viet propaganda). Such an answer would be controversial, but not groundless. The problem, however, is that this answer seems to contradict the core of Furet's undertaking. If he intended to write a history of the communist idea and of the illusion it generated—abstracting as much as possible from the history of political institutions, economical develop-ments, etc.—and concluding it with the year 1989, then he should have given a positive interpretation of the last forty-five years. The assumption that this period does not contribute anything to our understanding of the illusion, and is merely a consequence of what happened before, did not oblige him to wait until the institutional end of the system. The book in which Khrushchev's de-Stalinization is the last important development could have been written several years or even several decades earlier. If we follow the author's premises, the events of our times do not provide any substantial information about the end of Stalinism as an idea (though they do provide valuable information about the political and economic history of the earlier periods).

An analysis of the communist illusion in the post-Stalinist period, i.e., after the ideology of antifascism evaporated, would have been a difficult task. The communist idea was, at that time, less easily legible in the strate-gies of political parties, in philosophical books, and in the ideologies of communist societies and their elites. On the one hand, the ranks of com-munists have dwindled, and their programs have lost—as a result of the pressure of reality—some of the previous dogmatism; on the other hand, certain communist ideas (e.g., uncompromising anticapitalism) have be-come assimilated by other left-wing groups and ideologies, thus acquir-ing a touch of respectability. This explains why for quite a number of peo-ple the communist idea was never discredited sufficiently, or at least it was never as discredited as the fascist idea.

It also explains why the intellectual and ideological changes in the post-Stalinist period have not been well described. Oddly enough the failure to do so results from the same assumption we find in Furet's book. In Poland we have repeatedly heard a similar opinion voiced by many writers and public figures who have maintained that the genuine communist faith ended in 1956; afterwards, they say, we have had only opportunism, *realpolitik*, and inertia in politics and the sphere of ideas—socialism in the Western version that has little in common with the communist illusion. The effect of this opinion, both in Poland and in Western Europe (with some notable exceptions such as Alain Besançon), was a widespread belief that analyzing the scope and meaning of the communist idea no longer made much sense.

This weakness of Furet's book shows not only in failing to give a detailed account of one historical period. I think its consequence is neglecting questions and problems that inhered in Furet's initial argument and that could and should become a central object of his study. Let us compare his two statements, one from the beginning, the other from the end of the book. At the beginning he said that the revolutionary zeal was animated by strong antibourgeois and egalitarian sentiments. And this is what he said at the end referring to the situation of the modern man after the fall of communism: "He [modern man] rediscovers the complementary and contradictory elements of the liberal formula—human rights and market, and thus undermines the very essence of what has been the driving force of revolutionary messianism during the last two centuries. The idea of a different society is almost unthinkable today, and no one suggests anything that might anticipate a new conception. We are bound to live in the world in which we live." I find the transition from the first statement to the second arbitrary. In the course of the book we have not been given any hypothesis that would explain the decline of the revolutionary impulse after it became divorced from the communist idea. The internal conflict in the bourgeois mind was not removed, or at least Furet did not say anything about how it could have been removed: Both a desire for equality and outrage at existing inequalities continue to be predominant factors in modern political sensibility. It is therefore legitimate to ask in which direction this conflict, if it still exists, pushes the bourgeois soul today. How do the desire for a better world and a critique of the existing one express themselves today? How strong are the feelings of hate—new "antifascisms"—that appeared in the place of the weakened idea of communism and that were inspired by similar moral concerns?

Beginning his interpretation with an internal conflict in the soul of European bourgeoisie, Furet suggested he would outline what has been happening with this conflict from the time of its birth until today. But the moment he invoked the category of antifascism he lost sight of this picture and ignored all interpretational possibilities that inhered in it. In the concluding parts of the book he returned to it, however, this time suggesting—quite arbitrarily, to my mind—that the experience of the fall of communism helped to eliminate the conflict altogether. The conclusion is disappointing since it was not supported by any evidence, but came directly from his hypothesis that the actual end of the communist idea was the exhaustion of the ideology of antifascism. A reflection on the last four decades of communism would have been of crucial importance in identifying the missing element of the argument. Of course it would not have been a historical account in the strict sense, but rather an inquiry into the European soul at the time the communists were making the last, unsuccessful attempt to build their empire. As a historian Furet could have felt uneasy about that kind of inquiry, though there is no doubt that he was particularly qualified to this task.

The author, had he heard this critique, would probably have replied he had written a book about "the past of an illusion," not about "today's illusions." But such a reply would not have been satisfactory. With all due respect for Furet's mastery as an interpreter of history, we know quite a lot about the illusions from the earlier periods of the history of communism. We know considerably less about the illusions of the relatively recent past that continue to influence our perception of the world and that may be offshoots of the communist idea. Possibly what prevented Furet from writing about today's illusions was a generational difference. As he himself admits, the decisive year for him personally and for millions of people of his generation was 1956, to which date he also attributes the fall of the Great Idea. For younger people, however, the decisive year was 1989. An analysis of the illusions that preceded this date and probably will persist after it is still to be written.

8

Intellectuals and Communism

The role of intellectuals in inspiring and supporting the communist system has, for quite some time, ceased to be a matter of scholarly or journalistic interest. In the former communist countries the intellectuals actively participated in abolishing the regime, by which they have, or so it is believed, redeemed their old sins. Whether this redemption is really effective is debatable, but engaging in such a debate would not take us far. Many actors of that drama are no longer among the living, and those who are still with us react to every attempt at such a debate either with anger or with indifference mixed with condescension. This loud indignation or silent contempt characterizes not only former fellow-travelers but also the new generations of today's intellectual elite. A strong sense of generational community has emerged whose effect is the persistence of the old taboos: It is still not done to discuss certain discrediting facts from the past.

Invoking the problem once again, let us try to reflect on the deep involvement of intellectuals in the communist regime. This involvement had several forms: Intellectuals conceived the system, provided it with moral sanction, and participated in its institutions. To avoid misunderstanding, I reject at the outset two accusations that are sometimes heard. I do not accept the thesis that the presence of "armed prophets"—educated people who tried to give their ideas a political form—among the founders of the communist system could be turned against the intellectual class as a whole. Let us not forget that all or almost all movements in the human history were led by elites, and the communist movement is in no way exceptional; it, too, had at its peak a group people who turned from thinking to acting. Neither do I find convincing an accusation, formulated rather rarely, that intellectuals did not actively oppose the communist regime. To expect that they should have done so would be tantamount to demanding of them a heroic role and blaming them for not having fulfilled it. Such a criticism is dubious: One cannot accuse anyone of not being heroic, and should such an accusation be made, it would apply to all social groups.

The intellectuals should be criticized not because for many years they did not fight the system, but because they approved of it wholeheartedly. One cannot help feeling puzzlement that people who should see better and understand more than others became—more than others—liable to a deception that was, apparently, rather easy to see through. This deception refers not only to a few individuals but to a large number of the Western and Eastern intelligentsia; not only to mediocrities, but to the most illustrious representatives of arts and sciences; not for a brief period but for decades; not only in the countries with communist governments, but also in those societies that cherished civil and political liberties; not only with respect to the communist policies that were morally acceptable but also to the most hideous and inhumane forms of those policies; not only with respect to the idea of communism, but also to the actual policies of the Soviet Union, Red China, North Vietnam, Cuba, and even, improbable as it might seem, to Albania.

The question of how such an incredible attitude was possible is not a trifling one; it touches upon the fundamental weakness, moral and intellectual, of that particular social class that we call modern intelligentsia. History exposed this group to a serious trial that by and large they failed. The fact that a question of what went wrong is being raised less and less frequently today means that the intellectuals are no longer interested in their condition and have no intention of engaging in what may result in a painful reinterpretation of a sense of their mission.

The communist system was a child of the intellectuals in a far stronger meaning than, say, Nazism. Although in the case of Nazism one can discern some profound philosophical roots, but those artists, thinkers, and scientists who joined it did not do this primarily for intellectual reasons. Apart from Martin Heidegger whose philosophical links with Nazism are close but difficult to specify in unequivocal terms, the majority of those intellectuals who supported the system were motivated mainly by the belief that the era of parliamentary democracy was over and by a feeling of disgust towards existing culture; they were conspicuously less attracted by the ideas that the Nazi movement was said to represent. In a sense, Nazism was a product of political ideologues and leaders, not of intellectuals. It emerged without their participation, and only after it became a political force did it present itself to some intellectuals as a viable alternative to the current state of affairs.

The case of communism was different. It was probably the only modern political system totally invented by theorists and political prophets, and the support it managed to acquire was the greatest ever granted to any system in the political history of mankind. The affection the intellectuals felt for communism was, as it were, the affection for one's own child. No other regime had a similar status. Modern republicanism, just like the modern economic system, emerged through a long process of gradual adjustments and adaptations, and a theoretical reflection was never, so to speak, its efficient cause. What is more, the concept of communism did not come out of nothing, but had behind itself a long philosophical tradition with which the intellectuals were eager to identify themselves. This tradition oscillated around two ideas: revolution and humanism. The first idea implied a negative assessment of reality and a need to build it anew; the other justified the revolutionary venture by putting the good of man as the supreme value and his power and knowledge as the guarantee of success. Both ideas have substantially determined the intellectuals' way of thinking at least since the Renaissance, and there are no grounds to suppose this will change in the foreseeable future. In the world where a theocentric outlook has been marginalized, humanism seems to be the only universal moral idea left to politicians, moralists, and citizens.

It is often claimed that the first of these ideas, revolution, has exhausted its validity, because we are supposedly living in a postrevolutionary era. The claim is partly true and partly false. While it is true that both the intensity of the revolutionary spirit and its object have changed, the need for radical transformation has remained. The difference between our age and the "age of revolutions" is that the great transformation used to be primarily political and economic, whereas today it is moral, social, and cultural. But the difference is not decisive. The revolutionary spirit that set fire to the old regimes had its roots in the basic paradigms of modernity, and those paradigms, as I understand them, have not been replaced by the new ones. The idea of revolution still inheres in the way the modern intellectual thinks. Even if sometimes it fades away and acquires somewhat anachronistic connotations, it is still radical change, not continuity, that seems the natural interpretative pattern for the majority of the intellectual class. Change is natural and obvious whereas continuity requires justification. Those who do not think in terms of reforming the status quo put themselves in an unenviable position of those who accept the existing discriminations, inequalities, and other reprehensible practices.

For several centuries each epoch has defined itself through the works of its prophets and leaders, not only by opposing the epoch that preceded it but also by claiming its revolutionary role in the entire human history. The

enthusiasts tended to see in every turn of history a fundamental reorien-
tation, an absolute beginning that was to push humanity in a new direction and permanently change the destiny of man and the nature of human
order. This belief persisted in the Renaissance, in Cartesian philosophy, in
the Enlightenment; a revolution was proclaimed by the Romantics, and a
new beginning by the positivists. That the world will enter a new mag-
nificent era was predicted by the classical liberals and, quite recently, by
the champions of counterculture. Even our own epoch—seemingly devoid of illusions, particularly the illusions of progress—has also generated the ideas of the end of philosophy and metaphysics, after which, we
are told, a new culture of total disenchantment will emerge. The vision of
communism as a radically new stage in the human development was one
of many of that kind—not the first, and most certainly not the last one,
and perfectly accorded with this pattern of thinking.

   This does not imply, of course, that philosophical radicalism contains,
in itself, potential acceptance of communism, that in other words the revolutionary thinking of Descartes, Spinoza, Comte, and other great
philosophers is to be blamed for the massive attraction of intellectuals to
communist ideology with all its disastrous consequences. Such an assertion, historically and philosophically arbitrary, would weaken the personal responsibility of individual persons and would lead to an excessive
politicization of philosophy. What I do maintain is that a tendency to intellectual revolution characteristic of almost every philosophical orientation in the history of modernity might have resulted in a state of mind
which was not only sympathetic to political and economic revolutions but
in a way expected them. Radicalism of thinking does not, in itself, bring
about destructive practical consequences, not does it easily transform itself into a blueprint for political change. One can think of such intellectual
giants as Copernicus, Descartes, and several others whose theoretical radicalism coexisted with conservatism or moderation in the realm of practice. When, however, such radicalism reappears in virtually every orientation, cultural movement, and school of thought, one may suspect that
one has discovered a deeply rooted predilection of the modern mind. Although there may be—in fact there are—thinkers who do not succumb to
it, this predilection has a remarkably large representation among the intellectual class.

   The impact that the idea of revolution had on the modern mind is best
documented not only by the widespread support given to the Bolshevik
revolution by writers, thinkers, artists, scholars, and journalists; even
more remarkable is the insufficiently noted fact that this revolution was
also supported by the critics of the Bolshevik regime, including some of
the best known ones, which in turn considerably weakened the critique
they formulated. One can see it in the works that acquired an almost leg-

endary reputation in this respect: André Gide's and Bertrand Russell's. The reception of both had the atmosphere of a scandal, and both were later praised as landmarks of honesty and courage. Yet read today they seem rather modest manifestations of common sense. The reader is struck by a surprisingly great number of reservations Gide and Russell make to exclude possible misunderstandings—primarily that they had retreated to the position of the apologists of capitalism, or that they had condemned the socialist idea as such, or that they had failed to see the greatness of the revolutionary act. They probably wished to dissociate themselves from those weak minds to whom the protagonist of Stefan Żeromski's *Przed-wiośnie* reproachfully directed the question, "Do you have the courage of Lenin to start everything anew, to destroy the old and to build the new?" (the author of these words, let us note, could under no circumstances be called a fellow-traveler). The critiques of communism whose words sounded clearly and contained no such reservations—like George Orwell's—were few. The authors who were consistently anticommunist were not treated seriously: "a group of miserable blockheads," as Czesław Miłosz put it in his letter to Melchior Wańkowicz. Contempt was sometimes accompanied by ostracism (as in the case of Raymond Aron and Albert Camus in France) or by slander, ridicule, and moral annihilation (as in the case of Whittaker Chambers in the United States).

The second idea that underlay communism and survived it is humanism. Communism, however grotesque it sounds today, was conceived and constructed for the whole of humanity. Although in practice the political system turned out to be a failure—which today is not doubted by anyone, but not long ago such a statement would be considered a blasphemy or at least a pathetic form of defeatism—the moral idea of humanism was left untouched. It has been inextricably incorporated in Western culture for the last several centuries, and there are no signs it will wither away. This idea is, despite numerous and profound differences among many intellectual orientations, the only ethical principle that seems to be shared by all. As all-encompassing philosophical systems have declined, reality has grown increasingly disenchanted, and belief in the moral meaningfulness of nature has disappeared, the idea of humanism is the only message that has withstood the onslaught of the modern spirit of doubt and suspicion.

It is significant that the idea was found attractive both among those who professed triumphant Prometheism and among those who had strong reservations about human nature and its possibilities, bordering sometimes on nihilism. The slogans of humanism were dear to the thinkers of the Renaissance, to Marxists, to the progressives of the Enlightenment, to some romantics who believed that man can achieve great things and take the place of God. But it was also dear to skeptics and ironists, to reductionists and philosophers of suspicion who made their reputation on debunking the lofty ideals. Both of these attitudes were reflected in the reception of communism. That among the apologists we find a host of Promethean believers in the infinite perfectibility of man is quite understandable. We have, however, another group at least as numerous who cherished none of those illusions and whose presence in the procommunist front is therefore more puzzling. How can one explain the enthusiasm for communism of such authors as George Bernard Shaw, André Breton, André Gide, Jean-Paul Sartre, who by no means could be qualified as Permetheans? Oddly, among the unshakable supporters of the most brutal regime in history were people reputed for being refined demystifiers, dissident and rebellious, ironical and derisive, eager to strip away all philosophical, religious and ideological claims. All of them not only accepted the system, but seemed to espouse the humanistic message of communist propaganda.

How this was possible we do not really know. There are several explanations, none entirely satisfactory. One has been already mentioned. Humanism, beside being an expression of ideological faith, was also a platform for fighting against the hated status quo. Demystification, a prerequisite of this fight, became a passion so intense that it made the intellectuals dismiss the monstrosities of the new system. Contempt for "the old" was so fierce and uncompromising that it was often mistaken for devotion to the cause of man's emancipation, that is, to the cause of humanism that, it was believed, would naturally triumph in the wake of the destruction of the old order: The Voltairean slogan *écrasez l'infâme*, which was to recur in many variations throughout the nineteenth and twentieth centuries (from Ibsen to Girodoux and Brecht) and to fuel destructive energy into political ideologies, was perceived as easily translatable— through a simple reversal—into a positive notion of the good of mankind. The idea of humanism thus became linked to the idea of revolution. The hatred towards "the old" articulated in the postulate of revolution or in its apology deprived humanism of its former Promethean sentimentalism; humanism was no longer a domain of dreamers and visionaries, and became a difficult, even brutal, but necessary task to be achieved with the use of the appropriate means. Revolution, without this demystifying work of philosophers and artists, would remain intellectually immature, while the humanistic horizon, however distant, gave their work a moral sanction.

To what extent the intellectuals believed that the ultimate humanistic goal morally justifies the brutality of revolution, and to what extent they used the humanistic rhetoric cynically, we cannot be sure. Different authors suggest different interpretations. Some of the commentators went so

far as to argue that this humanistic background was pure mystification because the intellectuals were, down at heart, fascinated by the brutality of
the struggle against the old and by the beauty of revolutionary barbarism;
no one, save a few idealists, sincerely believed in the Arcadia of future
communism. This applied as much to the Western authors who observed
with satisfaction how a society was purged of social and cultural anachronisms, as it did to the Polish intellectuals who embraced communism because they could not think without disgust about the prerevolutionary
world; the world after the revolution, with all its drawbacks, had at least
the advantage of being free of the traditions of unreason. When the traditional moral ideals were believed to have collapsed, or as some would say,
were made to collapse as a result of the new ideas propagated by the
prophets of the revolution, a revolutionary act, longed for for so long, was
perceived as the only sensible, realistic type of political action.

This explanation sounds convincing, but it cannot be totally true. I
doubt the humanistic idea was simply a illusion or a ploy used by the intellectuals to sanction the brutal implementation of their projects. But it
cannot be doubted that this idea was elusive, and its elusiveness stemmed
primarily from the fact that that "man" in whose name communism was
conceived did not have a clear meaning. The intangible character of the
humanistic ideal was in a way convenient. It could induce the intellectuals to express solidarity with striking workers or landless farmers, but it
could also make them think in terms of, and give their support to, the
policies aiming at establishing the universal brotherhood of human beings; "man" could be a representative of the proletariat, a commissar, or a
hypothetical citizen of the future state of equality and justice. This jump-
ing from a concrete to an abstract, from an individual to a group, from reality to ideal, was frequent and in a way inevitable. Humanism could not
be closed in a clear and unequivocal formula because it inspired too many
aspirations and objectives.

This deeply felt but philosophically unclear message proved effective
not only during the communist era, when the crimes of communism were
being absolved or denied, but also after its demise, when absolution and
denial were no longer possible. Communism in its heroic stage was
deemed superior to capitalism even if in reality—as quite a few admitted—it offered less freedom and did not produce a comparable amount of
wealth. When communism fell, and the claims of a somewhat lesser degree of freedom and wealth under its regime could come only from the
mouth of communist dinosaurs, the humanistic idea once again came to
the fore, this time by preventing a large number of intellectuals from the
unconditional condemnation of communism.

Communism was no good—this much was granted—but it could under no circumstances be as bad as fascism. When in the early 1980s a

well-known American writer reputed for refined aestheticism (which
had not stopped her from writing an apologetic account of North Vietnam a couple of years earlier) called communism "a fascism with a human face," she made news headlines because she said something that
was morally shocking. A statement like this could be made by an unabashed cold warrior, but in the mouth of Susan Sontag it sounded like
intellectual provocation. But what shocked was only the first half of the
statement: about communism being equal to fascism. That communism
had "a human face" was markedly less controversial. A similar reaction
was observed in the commentaries to the *Black Book of Communism* published in France in 1997 when the reviewers, and even—which is particularly significant—some of its contributors, vehemently protested
against making those two system equal; their argument was precisely the
humanistic idea which however distant from the communist practice
had some ennobling effects. The moral source of communism remained
untainted.

Communism was thus not totally anathematized. The obstacles to its
unconditional condemnation have not disappeared, although today one
could not find many apologists of the Soviet Union, central planning, the
Gulag, or the dictatorship of the proletariat. Whenever the system is condemned, the condemnation is conditional: Those who say harsh words
about it are expected to say words at least as harsh about other systems
and institutions. The formulas vary: "the communist terror was evil but
America had senator McCarthy"; "communism meant a moral degradation of people, but nineteenth-century capitalism was also morally degrading"; "the communists had their gulag, but let us not forget that the
British and the Belgians had concentration camps in their colonies." Such
linkage does not exist with respect to Nazism. No one makes the condemnation of Auschwitz conditional on the simultaneous condemnation
of Kolyma; no one expects that we call the Nazi destruction of culture ab-
horrent only if we at the same time express our moral indignation at the
Stalinization of culture in Russia or Poland.

This ambiguous attitude toward communism is not a new phenomenon; it came into being in the 1950s when the facts about communist reality could no longer be questioned not because they were proven (that had
happened before), but because they were confirmed by the Soviet communists themselves. At that time there appeared an ideology that was to
be called anti-anticommunism; anti-antiNazism, let us point out, never
existed. The result of this new ideology was that anticommunism continued to be perceived as reprehensible, but this time for different reasons.
Previously it was criticized because the anticommunists turned against
communism as the highest achievement of humanism. Now their attitude
was no less condemned, but the reasons were more hinted than openly

formulated. It was suggested, and is still suggested, that some kind of spiritual affinity exists between a communist and an anticommunist, that, in other words, one should beware of anticommunism because it is a mirror reflection of its adversary. This led to a paradox: Communism was bad, but no matter how bad it was, anticommunism was never good. The people who had been supporting communism for many years became ready to admit they were wrong, but at the same time they directed their main critical impetus, as well as contempt, against anticommunists.

This phenomenon was widespread in the West, but it also had its equivalent in Poland just before and after 1989. In the West anticommunism was branded a form of servility towards the existing power structures, under the assumption that support for U.S. foreign policy was more discrediting than support for the policies of the Soviet Union, Vietnam, or Cuba. A considerable number of Polish intellectuals, loyal to the regime even during the time of its disintegration, considered themselves superior, in the new liberal democratic reality, to anticommunism and anticommunists, as if this reality was an organic offshoot of *Realsozialismus*, and not a result of its successful overthrow. For some reasons the long lasting apology of the Soviet system was viewed, not only by its functionaries and supporters but also by a large group of former oppositionists, as a civilizing experience, whereas in anticommunism they tended to see a form of barbarism. Of many examples I will mention only one: A widely read weekly, *Polityka*, which despite its consistently servile past has been always in good spirits about its being on the right side, and today is openly contemptuous toward anticommunism to the satisfaction—incomprehensible to me—of some of the regime's former victims.

In these reactions to communism one more factor must be mentioned: group conformity—a phenomenon well known in the history of intellectuals, but still somewhat puzzling and still vehemently denied. Whoever wanted to oppose the theory and practice of communism not only had to wrestle with difficult conceptual problems, but had to challenge a strong and complex network of mythological simplifications, prejudices, and stereotypes that united the intellectuals as a group. To put it simply, one cannot understand the intellectuals' involvement in communism without taking into account the phenomenon of conformity and, at the same time, without giving credit to the value of nonconformity; those who resisted this involvement had to take upon themselves a task of opposing the aggressive mythologies produced by the powerful propaganda machines of the Soviet Union and its satellites, but first of all they had to resist a far more difficult mythology, that of their own class. That it was easier to oppose the former than the latter is best shown by the fact that few were able to do it. The best known example is George Orwell, who was consistently and uncompromisingly struggling against the stifling ideas of his own intellectual milieu at the time when its pressure was particularly strong and when the lies it propagated had no parallel.

Why the intellectual class is susceptible to stereotypes no less than other social groups is a problem worth analyzing in itself, but it goes beyond the scope of the present essay. Let me point out only one reason. The intellectual class, we often forget, has a hierarchical structure: Only a few create ideas and formulate arguments; the overwhelming majority satisfy themselves with commenting on or imitating what others have said. The serious errors committed by the greats are thus hardly ever the subject of the reflection that could lead to a correction, because those errors perpetuate themselves through a process of imitation and exert a powerful impact on the whole group. The error in question, defending communism in theory and practice, was therefore never restricted to a statement by a particular writer, or thinker, or artist; it was always followed by the supportive opinions of lesser writers, thinkers, and artists, amplified and publicized by the press, strengthened by publishing policy, and even fostered by a system of education. The errors quickly transformed themselves into an intellectual machine that perpetuated a certain set of stereotypes and made the defense of communism immune from any forms of intellectual or moral subversion.

There was in fact a two-way process. On the one hand, the erroneous ideas of the greats were an inspiration to lower ranks, including mediocrities, who turned these ideas into social facts. On the other hand, those social facts had paralyzing effects, because they hindered an exchange of ideas by delegitimizing any challenge to the accepted axioms. This is why the dynamics of intellectual fashions and fascinations did not correspond to the dynamics of historical developments. Those developments could conclusively testify to the evil nature of communism, but this did not, automatically, translate itself into widespread philosophical reorientations. Radical conversions from communism to anticommunism—those that made the news headlines—referred to a relatively small number of people. The rest reacted rather conservatively, making modest modifications of a few theses, adding several qualifications, but retaining the overall perspective. There is a certain paradox in the fact that political radicalism as an intellectual position does not itself undergo radical changes, but rather is the subject of reactionism and inertia.

The above explains an ideological continuity of the Western intellectual class. The liberalization of communism in the late 1950s—which occurred as the Communist Party of the Soviet Union was officially confirming the regime's criminal record at the Twentieth Party Congress—had only short-term effects. Ten years later the Western world experienced an explosion of political radicalism during which communist and quasi-communist slogans reemerged with a new force, the memories of the past having apparently been almost completely wiped off. The new optimistic radicalism not only reawakened a wave of affectation for China, Cuba, Albania, and North Vietnam, but also led to new phenomena in politics—such as the idea of unilateral disarmament—and in intellectual life—such as historical revisionism defending the postwar foreign policy of the Soviet Union. All these novelties would have been impossible if it had not been for the intellectual bureaucracy with its in-built system of ideological preferences. In the 1960s professors and writers eagerly identified themselves with new slogans, although previously they had not shown any intention to man the barricades. When the young radicals, inspired by the teaching of the old masters, finally appeared and rushed to build such barricades, the university professors supported them in the belief that the leaders of the students' rebellion had restored the tradition of the revolution in the name of humanistic ideals.

It should thus be no longer surprising that the great events in the history of communism that objectively discredited the system failed to substantially decrease its popularity among the intellectuals. From the Moscow trials and the Ukraine famine, through the Ribbentrop-Molotov pact, the Katyn massacre, the subjugation of Central Europe, Khrushchev's secret speech, Budapest 1956, Prague '68, China's cultural revolution, and Solzhenitsyn's *Gulag Archipelago*, to Solidarity and the *annus mirabilis* of 1989, we have had, on the one hand, the slow disintegration of communist orthodoxy and the falling off of its dedicated adherents, and on the other, the gradual strengthening of leftist thinking and the spreading of anti-anticommunism. The more the real nature of communism became undeniable, the more reasons have been discovered to exonerate the ideas and the people that animated the movement politically and intellectually. A gigantic effort has been and is still being made to defend communism against itself.

This process is in no way puzzling once we remember the sociology of the intellectual class. Strictly speaking, this class is not an elite, if that word denotes a group of people with exceptional intellectual and artistic potential that imposes on them certain duties toward the whole society. The problem is not only that the real elite was a minority whereas the not-so-great intellectuals were a majority. For some time, this majority has been extremely numerous and growing in number, which practically undermines its elitist status. With the widening of education, the intellectual group has acquired an almost mass character, far exceeding the proportions one can reasonably grant to an elite understood as an aristocracy of intellect and imagination. Hence the group's behavior does not consist only in imitating the opinions, possibly mistaken, of the distinguished few, but also resembles typical reactions of a large group such as mimicry, acquiescence, assimilation. The choices made by the intellectual class, in short, are better explained in terms of sociological categories than in terms of the intellectual categories that explain relations between ideas. In our times the size of this group is sufficiently large to exclude a phenomenon of frequent ideological conversions under the pressure of experience or argument.

For some time we have witnessed a surprising discrepancy between the way the intellectuals behave and the ideas they proclaim. Their behavior is based on group conformity and the continuity of political preferences, whereas the ideology they espouse praises revolution, nonconformity, and disobedience. This dual nature of the intellectual also played some part in the reception of communism. The communist was usually—and to a degree still is—associated with an attitude of rebelliousness, which made him an object of sympathy. If he was a member of the communist party but out of power, he deserved sympathy as someone who was for the people against the unjust regime. If he himself was a functionary of this regime, he still could attract some sympathy: He represented—to recall the usual justification of Soviet leaders—a modernizing factor against the unjust structures generated by tradition. Expressing sympathy for communists and communism seemed to ennoble the intellectuals, because such an act put them in a situation of rebels or at least of oppositionists. In the communists—just as in anarchists, radicals, hunveibins, hippies, red Khmers, or eccentrics—they saw a partial realization of their own dreams and a reflection, however dim and imperfect, of their own ideal. But the dream of revolution—distributed among the ever increasing number of the intellectuals, filtered through the group stereotypes, through the stability of their own existence, through the bureaucratic structures of universities, media, and corporations, through informal networks of hierarchies and dependencies—turned into its negation and resulted in party-like homogeneity. The emergence, growth, and ultimate fall of communism changed little in these practices.

So far we have referred predominantly to Western intellectuals and their attitude to communism. How did the Polish intellectuals differ? What made the difference was, of course, their situation. For Poland's intelligentsia communism was not a distant reality that one could visit when invited by the government-controlled organizations of writers, artists, or peace activists, and look at from the perspective of a table full of vodka and caviar. This reality was genuine, and even those who were infatuated with ideology could not ignore it. Hence we ask a different question about Polish intellectuals' involvement in communism from the one asked about their Western colleagues' involvement; namely, how could those intellectuals support the system whose moral and economic bankruptcy was an integral part of everyday experience?

This question has two major answers. The first was given by Czesław Miłosz in his *Captive Mind* half a century ago, where he argued that the acceptance of communism had a philosophical nature. Polish intellectuals were convinced Western culture was coming to an end dictated by historical necessity that, they believed, expressed itself in communism. The second answer was given by those who criticized Miłosz—Gustaw Herling-Grudziński and Zbigniew Herbert being the best known—and who claimed that the support of communism did not result from an intellectual formula but from fear of communist terror. This terror was both the cause and the effect of all the intellectuals did, of their lies, denunciations, servility, cruelty, moral and intellectual degradation, lust for power, etc.

Before I comment on each of those hypotheses let me note that both—obviously—partly exclude each other, and both—less obviously—partly overlap. They exclude each other because according to the first one the intellectuals supporting the system did not know what it was, whereas according to the second one they knew it well but supported it because they were forced or they out of their own will decided to do so. On the other hand, both hypotheses are partly related, because for intellectuals more than for other groups intellectual error is directly linked with a moral error.

This last argument has been less frequently raised today. Some tend to deny it by suggesting that the whole society joined the system; so the intellectuals are in no way exceptional in their shameful acts. But this explanation is hardly convincing. Contrary to what is claimed today, collaborating with communist institutions was different from collaborating with communist ideology. People who joined the ranks of the communist party could and did find shelter from communist ideology at home, in family life and in their own mental or artistic life. This splitting of existence into two parts, one official and the other strictly private, did create a most demoralizing situation, but on the other hand it enabled a lot of Poles to keep intellectual sanity and to separate, at least psychologically and conceptually, truth from falsehood. Workers, engineers, or doctors (but teachers in a significantly lesser degree) could live two lives, public and private. The first was all lie; in the second there could be some truth.

The intellectuals' misfortune was that they had only one life. If a poet wrote a poem praising the genius of Joseph Stalin or was convincing people about the value of the Polish-Soviet friendship, he seemed in the eyes of the reader to engage the whole of his soul in the poetic message. All those whose occupation was based on conveying meaning through words and through self-expression and who used words and self-expression to justify the superiority of communism could not live the second life: After all, the writer is what he writes, and there is nothing else he can, as a personality, stand for. The intellectuals gave communism, sincerely or not, much more of their own deep selves than people of other occupations. The error they committed, if it was an error, turned out to be quite costly: They deprived themselves of that small margin of freedom, the freedom of the mind, which others managed to preserve in the private, almost secret spheres of their otherwise drab existences—the only place in those miserable times where truth and intellectual honesty could survive.

The communist intellectuals are sometimes defended with the argument that their philosophical decision to support the system, wrong as it was, resulted from a genuine sense of humanism. But the even if their humanism was genuine (which, as I have said, could be doubted), it does not provide a good defense because their erroneous decision had a destructive impact on other social groups that were trying hard to shield themselves against communist repressiveness. The intellectuals and artists were the only ones who could reach through that shield to the innermost feelings of other people without resorting to coercion. One could become immune to communist media and government propaganda; those who knew that communism was evil simply ignored official ideology. But it was far more difficult to defend oneself against propaganda from distinguished artists, writers, and academicians. A part of Julian Tuwim's genius that shone through his servile enunciations penetrated to the minds and hearts of his readers. The same was true of other poets, novelists, and philosophers who through their work first gained the sympathy and trust of the public and then deliberately used that sympathy and trust to attract people to the system that the majority of those people abhorred. The intellectuals who voluntarily sided with communism made people believe that communist ideology has some deeper meaning, some layer of wisdom that, like a treasure, is hidden beneath the ugly reality, and that those who lack education and sensitivity are unable to discern.

The sins of the intellectuals, even if they stemmed from philosophical rather than moral errors, go well beyond what they themselves said in support of the regime; they are also to be seen in how their words affected others. Today former communist intellectuals and their younger advocates often commend themselves for concrete acts of nonconformity that, despite their formal loyalty, they claim to have been able to make, or for the allegedly good balance of the game they were playing with the system. They seem to be unaware of the real damages for which they were responsible, not only in the case of culture or academic life, but also in the case of particular people. Those engineers of the human soul, as Stalin called them, intended to interfere with people's deepest convictions, that is, with the only sphere that provided protection against ideological aggression for those who were forced to live in the communist system. They try to put moral disorder into people's minds by infusing them with doubts and suspicions; they used their artistic and intellectual reputation to deprive people of an elementary sense of certainty that good is good and evil is evil; and last but not least, they undermined people's hope that comes from the belief that evil cannot have on its side those who possess wisdom and create beauty.

Both hypotheses—Miłosz's on the one hand, and Herling and Herbert's on the other—deserve more attention than they were given; both have important consequences for the present times. Let me start with the first one.

Despite the popularity of *The Captive Mind*, Miłosz's hypothesis was never a subject of a serious public debate, and there were, to my knowledge, no attempts to verify it. We do not really know how many intellectuals were lured by the notion of historical necessity and to what extent this notion affected people's perception of communist reality. *The Captive Mind* interested Polish readers less because of its original hypothesis and more because of Miłosz's psychological portraits of four distinguished Polish writers who had become ardent apologists of the system. A lot of attention was also given to *ketman*, a concept that undoubtedly added some dignity to the not so dignified activities of the intellectuals, which could be henceforth seen as a political and intellectual game; the game could be lost, to be sure, but the mere fact that they risked playing it was an evidence of their inner courage.

The problem with Miłosz's hypothesis is not only whether it can be verified; I, for one, tend to think that it describes the author's own philosophical dilemmas and his obsession with historical inevitability, rather than the attitudes characteristic of large segments of the Polish intelligentsia in the postwar period. The more important problem lies elsewhere. If the intellectuals' involvement in communism derived from an intellectual error, then one would expect that this error would sooner or later be corrected. It would, in other words, be natural to expect that an analysis of this error, and consequently, an analysis of communism, would be a major preoccupation of and a challenge to the Polish intellectuals in the coming years. This was not to be the case. Reflections on communism did not produce many works, and those few books that came out were written mostly by émigré writers. Therefore, if our men of letters and of academia committed an intellectual error that led them to become involved in the communist system—unfortunately, not a rare phenomenon in the twentieth century and hardly limited to Central and Eastern Europe—then the question of why they failed to reflect upon it is at least as interesting as why they had committed it. After all, a critical analysis of one's own errors seems a standard intellectual reaction of anyone who cherishes rational thinking. That such an analysis was not undertaken must lead us to conclude that Polish intelligentsia either do not admit having committed an intellectual error, or do not yet grasp its nature.

Whichever of these alternatives is correct, one can understand the consequence of this, the consequence that apparently no one in Poland, except the present writer, finds deplorable; namely, that once communism fell, it ceased to be of any philosophical interest to Polish intellectuals. Hardly anyone makes it his own object of study, and one has an impression that the communist experience no longer inspires the creative imaginations of artists and the minds of thinkers; it is now viewed as something closed, tedious, intellectually sterile, something that only obsessed and crude minds can take interest in. Those who know little about Poland and would like to reconstruct our experience of the past few decades from what they could find in our contemporary literature would never guess that we had been living under communist rule for almost half a century and that we got rid of the system only recently. When communism existed, the intellectuals did not analyze it because they could not: There was censorship, the sources were inaccessible, etc. Since the system fell, the intellectuals—with the notable exception of historians—do not analyze it, because it has ceased to exist. What is more, we have developed our own version of anti-anticommunism, one that resembles its Western equivalent. Having lived through different historical circumstances, a number of Polish intellectuals came to a similar state of mind in which they delegitimized the problem of communism and surrounded it with an atmosphere of hostility and suspicion.

This opting for the future ("opting for the future" was, by the way, the campaign slogan of the postcommunist candidate in Poland's last presidential election) by our intellectuals has another negative side: By refraining from analyzing the philosophical error they have lost an opportunity to contribute something significant to the problems that I think are central to the whole of Western culture. If we accept that communism has deep roots in our European heritage and if, as I suggested earlier, the spirit of revolution and the idea of humanism continue to affect today's thinking, then by avoiding any analysis of philosophical links between communism and our culture Polish authors have declined to participate in an important drama of modernity—or they admitted having nothing to say. Our collective experience, though most significant as material for philosophical reflection, is thus being wasted. Admittedly, the present times are not particularly conducive to such analyses, and it is possible a lot of potential writers have simply yielded to the dominant atmosphere and intellectual fashions. Whatever the reasons, one should regret that so little has been done to illuminate the error whose consequences still loom large, and thus little has been achieved in terms of illuminating the intellectual foundations of communism. Miłosz's book is practically the only statement in this respect.

The other hypothesis—which explains the intellectuals' collaboration with communism as an effect of terror and moral degradation—is, in a way, more convenient for the intellectuals. One could argue that in unusually demanding situations people do not behave impeccably and that once a certain level of political rationality is restored those same people will show a better part of their nature. This hypothesis would discredit the thinkers and artists morally—and like all people guilty of morally reproachable acts they might hope for forgiveness—but it would not discredit them intellectually; they were aware of the evil nature of the system but were terrorized and forced to do things they did not internally accept. In a system of freedom they would have behaved differently.

But this interpretation is being received with even less enthusiasm than the previous one, and not only on account of its obvious weakness; namely, minimizing the intellectual factors that played a role in the collaboration with the communist regime. For two reasons it is hard to imagine that this element was totally absent for the intelligentsia: First, communism was also wholeheartedly accepted by Western intellectuals who were not subject to terror; second, when the terror disappeared, sympathy with communism still existed.

The intellectuals reject this hypothesis because in general they are not willing to analyze their behavior in terms of moral degradation and guilt. Those few recent books depicting the moral pettiness of communism's supporters have been received with open hostility. When Zbigniew Herbert in his interview ten years ago spoke bluntly about his fellow writers' activities in the Stalinist era, almost everyone took offense, and some were outraged. The writers resented both the form and the content of his statement, though they did not deny any particular accusation. As I've said, the strongest argument justifying their outrage is the claim that they redeemed their sins by taking part in the democratic opposition against the system in the late 1970s and 1980s.

The 1980s will indeed be remembered as the time when the intellectuals fulfilled their duties in an exemplary way: They did not accept martial law in culture and became actively involved in clandestine educational and publishing activities. In this otherwise depressing period, the intellectual life gave people hope and became a bastion of resistance that strengthened all those who participated in it, morally as well as spiritually. The beneficial consequences of artists' and thinkers' involvement in underground culture cannot be overestimated, and one cannot help being impressed by the courage of people—a few at the beginning in the 1970s, and growing in number in the next decade—who risked repression by opposing communist ideology as well as the institutions it served.

But the Polish intelligentsia also met with some criticism at that time. The critics claimed that the resistance was in fact a purely moralistic gesture and did not result in intellectually independent thinking and a serious exchange of arguments. Philosophically, it was sterile and therefore did not generate important contributions to our understanding of communism. Moral rejection of the regime and its ideology—undoubtedly genuine—was inspired intellectually by ideas that emerged not from the Polish experience, but rather from the books of Western philosophers (from Hannah Arendt to Alain Besançon), without contributing any substantially new insights—if one does not count that emotional intensity that feeds itself on simplifications. This emotional intensity, not philosophical understanding, had cathartic effects for those intellectuals who had supported communism in the past. They now felt free of their own sins and reacted angrily to every attempt to analyze their past record. The analyses of those sins were dismissed as having little informative value and sometimes were even compared to "pornography."

The few books that did come out with the intention of giving some inside perspective of the intellectuals' involvement were on the whole disappointing, although they undoubtedly contained much interesting material. Some of the writers who were interviewed said, amazingly, that they saw a moral continuity between being involved in communism and being involved in the anticommunist opposition. In both cases, they maintained, there was the same desire to help people, the same humanistic impulse to make the world better, the difference being only in the ultimate end, not in the moral motivation. Those authors apparently confused the continuity of their own psychological identity with the continuity of their moral acts. If they sincerely believed that such a moral continuity existed, and that the opposition to communism had behind it the same moral motivation as procommunist enthusiasm, then not only did they undermine, unwittingly or not, their own admirable stance in the 1980s, but they seemed to pose as moral simpletons unable to go beyond repeating the moral simpleton's favorite formula that he meant well.

This escape from the charge of moral degradation into moral naïveté, and thus also into innocence, is not only unconvincing, but it disqualifies the intellectuals' later moral positions. Assuming that the support for communism was ultimately an incidental consequence of a strong and essentially right moral motivation, we are bound to assume that the resistance to communism was also an incidental consequence of the same strong and essentially right motivation. If the impulse to resist communism and the impulse to support it were both expressions of humanism, then we come to the conclusion that confirms what has been said before: The humanistic impulse is unpredictable, and we do not know in which direction it will turn in each tide of human history. Observing today's life, in Poland and elsewhere, we cannot doubt that among the intellectuals this impulse will not weaken in the future and it continues to drive them to ever new causes. One cannot be sure, however, if in the not so distant future they will be willing to accept the consequences of their present involvements.

9

✢

Sir Isaiah Berlin:
A Naïve Liberal

Isaiah Berlin's high position in the Anglo-American philosophical world is something of a mystery. For many years philosophy in Britain and in the United States has been dominated by the analytical approach; everything that did not satisfy this criterion was treated with an almost unconcealed contempt and classified as inferior from the perspective of scholarly standards. If we were to assess Berlin in this light, he should not be called a philosopher, not even a scholar. In his long life he wrote only one book—Karl Marx's intellectual biography published in 1938. The rest of his writings are essays, *pièces de circonstances* as he himself used to called them, and among those only a few—and less well-known ones at that— could be considered strictly philosophical; they were later published in a volume entitled *Concepts and Categories* with a foreword by Bernard Williams. Perhaps one more item deserves to be included among Berlin's scholarly works: his anthology of the Enlightenment philosophers with a running commentary. But it is not these works that made Berlin famous. What brought him international prestige and fame were his essays, not scholarly in the strict sense of the word, not even consistently philosophical, but rather focusing on a history of intellectual and artistic culture.

How Isaiah Berlin managed to achieve such a reputation among the philosophers, even among the orthodox adherents of the analytic school, I do not have a satisfactory explanation. There are probably several reasons. Although Berlin represented everything that his colleagues, as a rule, looked down on, they must have nevertheless admired his brilliance, erudition, versatility, art of conversation, and the beauty of his style. He was not just a learned professor, but rather a most

135

successful combination of two intellectual traditions: that of Russian intelligentsia and of the British university gentlemen as described by Cardinal Newman in his *Idea of a University*. With the first Berlin shared a love of ideas and a conviction that those ideas have an impact on reality; with the second, sympathy for philosophical empiricism and distrust towards all-encompassing systems. It is perhaps these traits of the intellectual temperament, reinforced by his power of personality, that made the analytical philosophers—usually intellectually ascetic, ahistorical, and therefore prone to philosophical sterility—recognize Berlin's rank as well as the quality of his mind. He was, as the East Europeans would put it, a man of culture in the most genuine, profound, and fascinating sense of the word.

We cannot understand Berlin's career unless we have a knowledge of Oxford University, not necessarily as an intellectual center, but rather as an institution as such with its rules, practices, politics, and game of interests. This world is not sufficiently transparent and legible for an outside observer, and one should not venture risky hypotheses about academic careers. It should be noted, however, that many observers said that Berlin fit well into the Oxford left-wing establishment, and although he did not always identify himself with the prevailing views, he occasionally supported them and received support in turn. This alliance was often interpreted in philosophical terms (shared hostility toward conservative and right-wing ideas, for instance), but sometimes in terms of opportunism and the imperatives of internal politics. Whatever the reasons, some of Berlin's actions were hard to reconcile with his humanistic liberalism and the spirit of nonconformity, but they accorded very well with the logic of power, providing him not so much with philosophical followers as with a political base. One example: Berlin actively supported giving a prestigious position (the Chichele Chair of Social and Political Theory) to G. A. Cohen, a Canadian-born scholar who until 1989 considered himself a Marxist and who prior to the appointment had published only one book, a defense of Karl Marx's theory of history.

Berlin's readers, especially outside Britain, were less interested in Oxford politics and more in the intellectual quality of his writings, not necessarily evaluated from the analytical point of view. The question, then, is whether the reputation he gained was justified and whether it will stand the test of time. My answer would be that Sir Isaiah was an extraordinary personality, but as a thinker he should be classified among the average. This judgment may seem brutal under the circumstances—his recent death, which usually inspires apologies, and the legend that has been built around him during the last half century. It is reasonable, however, if only we free ourselves from the apologetic aura and look at Berlin's writings in a more disinterested manner.

Let us begin with the laudation. Berlin's essays have unique features that make them impossible to imitate, from the literary style—those long sentences, interrupted by numerous asides and interjections, full of adjectives and other qualifications—to the exposition where philosophical argumentation is intermingled with biography, historical facts with references to literature, music, or paintings. Each of these essays is in a way a work of art; it is an intellectual narrative or, better, an intellectual drama that has a clear and intriguing plot. Some of those plots have become famous: for instance, Giambattista Vico as a thinker who anticipated the organismic and antirationalist philosophy of Romanticism; Leo Tolstoy as a fox, not a hedgehog (the former having a pluralist view of reality, the latter interpreting it in light of one organizing principle); Verdi as a naïve, not a sentimental, artist (based on Schiller's distinction between a "naïve" art of natural and spontaneous expression, and a "sentimental" art resulting from a conscious creative act that assumes a contrast between reality and idea); Joseph de Maistre as a precursor to fascism and Nazism.

Those stories narrated by Berlin have all the qualities of good literature: They are convincing and interesting, stylistically sophisticated, memorable and inspiring. They also constitute compact wholes that cannot be reduced to a structure of arguments and accordingly verified piece by piece. One cannot resist feeling that such an operation would destroy the subtle fabric of Berlin's work, just as a theatrical play would be destroyed once we try to reduce it to a system of syllogisms. This does not mean, of course, that Berlin's essays contain interpretations that are false or arbitrary. It is quite possible that Verdi was the last "naïve" composer, or that in Tolstoy there is more "fox" than "hedgehog." On the other hand, the picture of de Maistre as a forefather of Nazism seems definitely one-sided. At any rate, the overwhelming impression is that directing polemics against Berlin's essays would usually be inappropriate. When several years ago Mark Lilla wrote a splendid book on Giambattista Vico and tried to prove that much of what Berlin attributed to the Italian author was not there, he was virtually ignored. It is not only that the unusual reverence surrounding Berlin is not conducive to an exchange of arguments; a more customary reaction to his essays was and is either an aesthetic admiration for his intellectual vision, or their rejection in toto.

Berlin's essays have the beauty of an architectural work of art where the whole is subordinated to one principle that harmoniously organizes all the pieces—elements of philosophy, social history, art, literature, and other disciplines—into one unified construction. The essays show more the mind of a hedgehog than a fox, to apply Berlin's favorite distinction to himself. His mind was also "naïve" rather than "sentimental." The dominant principle cannot be severed from the objects it organizes and be analyzed independently; no clear theory stands behind it, no ideology, no sense of a contrast between the interpreted object of thought and a philosophical norm. Just as Verdi in the aforementioned essay was said to ignore the "sentimental" critics, Berlin seems indifferent to the philosophical scrupulousness of his adversaries. His writings are not the work of a disciplined and systematic mind that categorizes, discovers contradictions, and formulates hypotheses, but rather a product of a temper or a spirit (in the Romantic sense so often invoked by Berlin himself) that is a synthesis or in fact the most sublime form of cognition encompassing reason and heart, aesthetic intuition, moral sense, and practical intelligence, grasping the whole of the object in the mysterious act of perception.

All these characteristics, effective in the essays on art, aesthetics, and culture, are less admirable in the pieces focusing on ideas. The essays of the first type are fascinating for their richness and originality, while the essays of the second type seem schematic and secondary. Let us take as an example perhaps the best known and certainly the most influential of Berlin's texts, "Two Concepts of Liberty." It should be noted at the outset that there is not and in fact there has never been anything strikingly original in it, even at the moment it was published. The text received importance primarily from its social and political context, and also because Berlin was able to describe an old dichotomy with the forcefulness and clarity for which he was known. The essay, appearing in 1959, had as its context the Cold War. The apologists of socialism and communism—not only common propagandists but also the distinguished intellectuals of Western culture—were then arguing that the new Marxist regimes do not deprive man of freedom, but give him a freedom that is in essence truer, more profound, and more important. Berlin challenged this argument by showing the logic that underlies it and the deception it generates. He maintained that the idea of positive freedom where liberty means self-mastery, did not result from political manipulation but had a rich philosophical tradition behind it. The core of Berlin's argument was that, respectable though the idea of positive freedom was, it could easily be transformed into an intellectual sanction of serfdom.

The defense of negative freedom as a classical liberal notion had, at that time, a sobering effect. The same essay, however, read outside the historical context and especially at the time of a strong position of negative freedom loses its importance, and even shows too many and too obvious simplifications, a trait unworthy of a writer who was famous as a vigorous defender of pluralism.

One gains a similar impression reading Berlin's essay on historical inevitability, a notion brought to prominence with the popularity of socialism and communism and used indiscriminately. Socialism was believed to be a necessary outcome, whether one wanted it or not, of the inexorable laws of history. Today, however, with the Marxist faith in historical necessity faded, the essay seems rather sterile. We do not find in it any argument that, reformulated and modified, could make us somewhat skeptical about current beliefs in the inevitability of changes: for instance, the inevitability of modernization, the inevitability of Max Weber's *Entzauberung*, the inevitability of postmodernity, etc.

Berlin's theoretical texts not only have few original insights but also seem to illustrate typical liberal prejudices that we find in less subtle writers. In his critique of positive liberty one is first of all struck by the politicization of thinking that stems from a frequent use of the so-called slippery slope argument. If in any conceptual pattern or hypothesis one can find a potentially dangerous practical consequence, however remote, then this pattern or hypothesis becomes discredited because one is bound to believe that it has its own internal dynamics that, as if on a slippery slope, pushes it to the worst consequences. Thus when Berlin writes about those who divided the human nature into the higher and lower parts, that is, into the genuine Ego and the superficial Ego, he immediately shows that the distinction generates a political structure that in the name of man's higher and therefore genuine nature enslaves the lower and superficial one; when he writes about human consciousness as an inner citadel in which we find refuge against the vicissitudes of the outside world, he also says that this could create the conditions for the abolition of all the limits of political power; when he mentions Sarastro (from Mozart's *Magic Flute*) and Socrates, both of whom might symbolize the striving for the ideals of wisdom and excellence, he instantly feels obliged to add that in this striving there might be seeds of despotism, etc., etc. In effect one must conclude that a large area of thought, identified by means of one spacious and elusive category of positive freedom—covering such thinkers as Socrates, Plato and Aristotle, through the Scholastics, to Descartes, Kant, and Hegel—has been castigated as extremely dangerous and thus, whenever possible, to be avoided.

To be sure, such a tendency to create powerful demonologies and systems of taboos has been present in the liberal thought since the beginning, and its consequence—not always realized by the liberals themselves but clearly effective in liberal culture—has been to frighten the members of a liberal society with a specter of enslavement, thus hindering them from reflecting on serious problems that are supposed to be politically dangerous. I do not want to imply that Berlin totally identified himself with such a demonology. But he did show some inclinations toward it, which can be seen, for example, in his caricatural notion of monism that he associated with "faith in a single criterion" and opposed to the pluralism and humanitarianism of liberal civilization. Regardless of the fact that no serious thinker striving to give a unified picture of reality—not Plato, nor

Aristotle, nor St. Thomas Aquinas, nor Spinoza—ever believed in a single criterion, one cannot help being struck by the unfairness of Berlin's statement that attributes to metaphysical claims—on no grounds at all save perhaps persistent liberal prejudices as well as his own idiosyncrasies—primitive political content. To make the matter worse, he finished his essay on liberty with another unphilosophical statement, accusing the "monists" of being childish and immature. Even the language in which he articulated it shows the inherent unwillingness to treat the metaphysical propositions as something other than effects of one's practical intentions or, at best, psychological defects. "The very desire for guarantees," he wrote, "that our values are eternal and secure in some objective heaven is perhaps only a craving for the certainties of childhood or the absolute values of our primitive past."

Taken in isolation, such statements would deserve the criticism that they demonstrate more intellectual childishness and primitivism than any of the arguments formulated by the "monists." And yet the overall impression is that Berlin is less dogmatic than his fellow liberals. What prevented him from becoming a prisoner of those clichés were probably his intellectual qualities—subtlety of mind and philosophical culture—which made his simplifications appear less crude and more elegant than those of other liberals. I would say that he owes a lot to his "naïveté." A reader of Berlins's essays felt that the same arguments that sounded so irritating when stated in the versions of "sentimental" liberals could be treated as a record of intellectual experience, a reflection of the British philosophical tradition resistant to Continental rationalism, rather than a ready-made formula one could use to fight the philosophical enemies of liberty. Yet one cannot but feel disappointment that Berlin employed all his erudition and power of mind to make philosophical systems objects of fear and derision, instead of illuminating the problems that gave rise to the notion of positive freedom, for instance, or reflecting upon the higher and lower parts of human nature, or the role of consciousness as an inner citadel, or the role of moral virtues and ideals in modern societies—regardless of whether these problems indeed do or do not place us on a slippery slope at the bottom of which there is some form of enslavement.

In one of his essays Berlin wrote, perceptively and correctly, that the twentieth century has produced a peculiar way to cope with the difficult problems: Instead of trying to solve them we invalidate them by making suspect those who have raised them. To this bad practice not only the Marxists contributed but also the liberals, including—I say without pleasure—Isaiah Berlin himself. In today's world there is no better way to discredit the question than by indicating that the mere fact of raising it may, in an indefinite time and in indefinite circumstances, lead to the enslavement of someone by someone else.

About the Author

Ryszard Legutko is Professor of Philosophy at Jagellonian University.